SOLDIER'S SON

*To Mark — great guy,
better neighbor and best citizen
of our fair & friendly city.
May you enjoy these family
stories! All the best!*

Ben

7-30-07

SOLDIER'S SON

Ben McClelland

BEN W. McCLELLAND

UNIVERSITY PRESS OF MISSISSIPPI
Jackson

Publication of this book was made possible in part
through the support of the Lexington Foundation.

www.upress.state.ms.us

Designed by Todd Lape

The University Press of Mississippi is a member of the
Association of American University Presses.

12 11 10 09 08 07 06 05 04   4 3 2 1
∞

Library of Congress Cataloging-in-Publication Data

McClelland, Ben W., 1943–
Soldier's son / Ben W. McClelland.
p. cm.
ISBN 1-57806-625-5 (alk. paper)
1. McClelland, Ben W., 1943– 2. McClelland, Ben W., 1943–
—Childhood and youth. 3. McClelland, Ben W., 1943– —
Family. 4. McClelland, Ewing R., d. 1944. 5. Children of
military personnel—United States—Biography. 6. Soldiers—United States—Family relationships. 7. Prisoners
of war—Germany—Biography. 8. World War, 1939–1945—
Prisoners and prisons, German—Biography. I. Title.
CT275.M46533A3 2004
940.54'7243'092—dc22   2003016332

British Library Cataloging-in-Publication Data available

To all of my family,
those here and those gone before,
especially my father, Ewing Ray
McClelland, my mother,
Marianna Wright McClelland,
my brother, Ewing Richard
McClelland, and my twin sister,
Mary Jane McClelland Dooley

What, after all, is history if not
the words handed down through
remembrance and kindred blood?

—**WILLIE MORRIS**
Homecomings

CONTENTS

1

ACKNOWLEDGMENTS

This project has resulted from the collaborative efforts of many people. My brother, Pete McClelland, and my sister, Mary Jane McClelland Dooley, have been sources of primary documents, as well as aids to my memory. Each has participated in several conversations—in person and on the telephone—and has responded to e-mails, supplying vital information and many family anecdotes. My cousin Rosemary Wright Herring and my sister-in-law, Virginia Downer McClelland, have also been most helpful in locating photographs, in piecing together family information, and in reading early versions of the text. My uncle, James W. McClelland, helpfully answered many queries and supplied information on the McClelland and Frost families.

I have borrowed freely from the annotated family tree that my uncle Lloyd Austin Wright composed and sent to members of the Wright clan several years ago.

My colleagues David Galef, Colby Kullman, Cynthia Shearer, and Joe Urgo, all readers of early portions of the text, responded with fine insights and encouragement. My dear friend and colleague Anna Quinn has been an inspiring force for many years and helped me conceive of this work. Anna read and responded helpfully to several versions of the text; she also created opportunities for me to present portions of this work-in-progress to public audiences in Blue Mountain and in New Albany, Mississippi. Angela Elder-Quinn read and responded to the text and provided helpful suggestions on reordering the material.

Two of my children, Ryan and Brooke, also read early portions of the book, responded, and cheered me on.

My wife, Susan, who has been so busy with her own professional responsibilities, has provided both invaluable responses to the text and emotional support to me throughout my work on this project.

Susan, Anna, and my niece Amy Lynn McClelland provided me with warm companionship on a pilgrimage to my father's grave at the American Military Cemetery at Margraten, The Netherlands.

I owe a debt of gratitude to the University of Mississippi for support of my research travel and for use of its computer equipment and technical services. Eric Williamson produced visual material and engineered the audiotaping of segments of the text for public presentation. Several University of Mississippi librarians, including Amy Mark, assisted me in conducting research. Computer consultant Amelia Rodgers helped digitalize several documents and images; she also lent her expertise in troubleshooting technical challenges in producing an electronic text.

Many special friends and close colleagues from the National Writing Project—especially Nell Green, Cathy Stewart, and Rochelle Smith—also deserve recognition for helping me understand the power of writing to teach and to heal.

Many friends in AWON—American WWII Orphans Network—have assisted me in research and have enabled me to understand the national context of our lives. I'd like especially to thank those with whom I first met, including Adrian Caldwell, Ruth Malone, and Sondra Davis.

Finally, I want to thank the University Press of Mississippi, especially Craig Gill, who saw a book in the early manuscript, Anne Stascavage, who guided the book through the editing and production processes, Carol Cox, who edited carefully and fluently, and Walter Biggins, who handled logistics and communication.

Sources consulted in the preparation of this memoir include Andrew S. Hasselbring's "American Prisoners of War in the Third Reich" (Ph.D. dissertation, Temple University, 1990); Robert C. McClelland's *Masontown, Pennsylvania, and Its Environs: A Contribution to Their History* (Norfolk, VA: The Norfolk College of William and Mary, 1962); *Masontown: Sesqui-Centennial Celebration, 1798–1948*, edited by Sarah Wright, Mary Moxey, and Ann Ambrose (Masontown, PA, 1948); and "The Story of the 106th Infantry Division" (Army Education Services, written with the assistance of Commanding Officer Major General Donald A. Stroh and his staff). "A Cabin of Family Stories" was printed in an earlier version in *Writing Practice: A Rhetoric of the Writing Process* (New York: Longman, 1984).

SOLDIER'S SON

1

KILLED IN ACTION

Masontown, Pennsylvania
December 24, 1944–January 25, 1945

On Christmas Eve of 1944, Mom received a telegram reporting tersely that Dad had been missing in action since the seventeenth, the second day of the Battle of the Bulge. Try though she might, she could get no further information from the government about his fate. With a toddler and twin infants, Mom observed the holidays filled with dread and distress. Following weeks of worry, she returned on the first day of the winter term to continue teaching her second-grade class. For her, staying busy with her pupils' reading, spelling, mathematics, and penmanship was preferable to sitting at home waiting day after day. As one of the twins, I did not hear about this episode of Mom's life until years later when my cousin Rosemary, who was a pupil in Mom's class, recalled it.

One day in late January, Rosemary's mother, my aunt Rose, appeared at the classroom door with another telegram in her hand. One glance at Aunt Rose's grim face and Mom fainted. Aunt Rose helped Mom out to the car and drove her home.

WESTERN UNION
Washington, D. C.
Dated 1/25/45

To Mrs. MaryAnne W. McClelland
201 North Main Street
Masontown, Pa.

Report now received through the International Red
Cross that your husband 1st Lt. Ewing R. McClelland
who was previously reported missing in action was
killed in action on 23 December while a Prisoner of

War of German Government. The Secretary of war extends his deep sympathy. Concerning letter follows.

J. A. ULic.
Adjutant General

2

"DAD, IT'S BENNY"

*The American Military Cemetery
at Margraten, The Netherlands
August 2000*

More than fifty-five years after Mom received that second telegram, here I stand. Across acres of grass, white marble crosses fan out in curved rows, looking from above like so many gull wings arcing silently over the sea. In the center of these 8,302 crosses stands one. I turn into Plot J, step deliberately to the middle of Row 3, stop and peer intently at Grave 8. It hits hard now. Trembling, I look through tears—and through the memory of a gold star, of mothballs, and of parentheses—to a single cross: Dad's.

> EWING R. MC CLELLAND
> 1LT 589 FA BN 106 DIV
> PENNSYLVANIA DEC 23 1944.

Finally, with this pilgrimage, I am here, face-to-face with the fact of my dad's death. Even at age fifty-six, I feel like the child he left so long ago. In my mind I say, "Dad, it's Benny."

I can now count myself among those for whom he died. But what circuitous journey of half a century has brought me to this point, to this place of understanding? How has growing up without him—and with a war hero ghost, instead—affected who I am? In what ways has his death—and the way my family treated it—influenced my identity?

3

WHERE I(T) STARTED

Masontown, Pennsylvania

Located about seventy miles south of Pittsburgh on the Monongahela River, this southwestern Pennsylvania town has a long history. Area mounds reveal the presence of ancient inhabitants who antedated by thousands of years the native tribes that were established when the first Europeans arrived in the area. Area place-names refer to old Indian settlements and battles of the French and Indian War in our colonial history. George Washington, John Mason, Albert Gallatin, and Edward Braddock all trafficked here. In the early 1900s the burgeoning coal industry turned Masontown into a boomtown with several large mines dug into the surrounding hillsides, with Bessemer coke ovens reddening the night skies in the valleys at Nemacolin and Gray's Landing, and with coke-filled barges riding the muddy Monongahela waters to steel mills in Pittsburgh. In tribute to the main industry, the local newspaper, the *Klondike Bulletin*, sported a rectangular piece of coal as the logo in its banner—depicted as a glistening crystal, not a grimy lump. The region's annual festival crowned a young beauty as Coal Queen. While this industry supported thousands of families—many of whom came from the British Isles, southern Europe, and the Slavic countries—there were serious costs to pay. Mining was both hard and dangerous work. Besides risking their lives to occasional, disastrous explosions, workers also contracted respiratory diseases. Working the coke fields was also exhausting labor: workers endured intense heat, raking red-hot coke from gaping oven mouths. All workers and their families suffered through periods of lost work during, for example, the stagnated economy that followed World War I and the general strike in 1922. At the time ubiquitous smoke, ash, and coal dust were simply aspects of the landscape, not fully understood as environmental and health hazards.

Built on a series of hills and long, low bottoms, Masontown numbered about five thousand inhabitants when I was growing up there after World War II. The coal boom was slowly but inexorably going bust, turning Masontown into a quiet, if not yet economically grim, hamlet. Yet in the fall of 1948, the place brimmed over with civic pride that carried the town through a week of sesquicentennial activities. The celebration's publication of a one-hundred-page memorial booklet—edited by Aunt Sally and two of her teacher friends—featured a summary of the town's history, dozens of pictures, and lists and lists of notable people, athletic teams, and community groups.

My paternal grandfather was a pit boss in the mine. My maternal grandfather supervised the machine shop in the Ronco mine, until he disputed the Frick Coke Company management practices and set out on a long, successful career as a businessman, local politician, and civic leader.

Dad and Mom eloped on December 15, 1940, keeping it secret until the following summer. Years later, Mom told us that she sat at Gram's deathbed that winter, wanting so earnestly to tell her grandmother that she and Dad had married, but feeling that she couldn't possibly risk it. Having been unable to share her joy with the grandmother she loved so much bothered Mom always. Neither did she tell her mother, although Grandma Wright later said she had suspected it when Dad gave Mom a four-piece, mahogany bedroom suite for Christmas. When Mom's picture appeared in the newspaper in June, the article about "the charming bride" stated that the couple's friends and families were "quite surprised" to learn the news.

While Mom lived on army bases with Dad for short periods of time over four years of marriage, she really never left her family home. So, when Dad went to Europe in the fall of 1944, my mom, my older brother, my twin sister, and I lived at the Wright family home at 201 North Main Street with Pop and Grandma Wright. Dwelling there, as well, were my aunt Rose and two first cousins whose father, my uncle Tom, was overseas, too, in an ordnance division in France. The Wright home wasn't your typical bungalow. According to family lore, the Wrights had outgrown a small house at the north end of town three decades earlier. In 1916 Pop erected a two-story, brick building two blocks north of the town center, on the foundation of the town's first mill. The ground floor housed his business, a Ford dealership: two showrooms, an office, a parts room, and a repair shop. When Pop proposed to Grandma that they live above the business, she said, "I won't live there unless it has large windows." As a result they built extratall windows to let in plenty of light. The extended family lived in two separate apartments that spanned fifteen spacious rooms on the second floor.

A baby grand piano was the focal point of the living room. Pop had it hoisted by a crane and brought in through the window openings before the casements were built. Actually, as the story goes, Pop first had a full-size grand installed. Grandma cried when she saw how much room it took up, so Pop sent it back, replacing it with the smaller version. Even with a couch, a coffee table, a recliner, two stuffed chairs, a TV, and a stereo along with the piano, the large living room was an open and comfortable space. We never produced any concert pianists, although a number of family members tickled the ivories. Cousin Rosemary recalls Pop teaching her to sing a number of songs, and I can imagine him sitting on the long bench with Mom a generation earlier. However, we kids did hear sonatas and concertos masterfully performed by the piano's player mechanism. To tell the truth, we were more fascinated by the mechanical action of the player than we were by the musical sounds it produced. It seemed like magic seeing the scrolls of perforated paper roll through the player and cause the tiny brass tines to strike the piano wires.

Because my dad never returned from the war and because Mom never remarried, we remained at Pop's throughout my childhood and youth till I left for college. And so it was that we three McClelland kids weren't really raised as McClellands, as we would have been had we lived in a house with our mom and dad, but rather as Wrights, with a mother, grandparents, and three sets of Wright uncles and their wives—all of whom had a hand in our rearing. This may seem an unremarkable turn of fate. Of course, not until I was grown did I ever give it a thought, much less speculate about how I might have turned out differently had I been reared in a McClelland household. However, besides a marked difference in the temperaments of the families, the Welsh-and-English-descended Wrights had moved from the farm-and-laboring class to the mercantile-and-professional class a generation earlier than the Scotch-Irish-and-German-descended McClellands did. Besides, rather than living in a typical nuclear family arrangement, we moved about in a large, consanguineous family, headed by a long-popular businessman, political operative, and civic leader. Each of Mom's three brothers in his own distinctive way played a very active avuncular role.

As toddlers, we fell in with the pace of family members, nannies, cleaning ladies, deliverymen, and guests who bustled about the place day and night. Our home took on its own persona; we often referred to it by its address, "201" (pronounced "two-oh-one"). It resembled a rooming house, with large meals being served three times a day. On Mondays big-boned Ella worked in the laundry at the gas-heated mangle, pressing a heap of freshly laundered bedsheets and pants. A large exhaust fan in the window whirred noisily like an airplane propeller, but seemed little help in cooling that laundry on summer Mondays. In the evenings a crowd of folks gathered around the radio console in Pop's radio room, listening to the evening news and to programs such as the one featuring Charlie McCarthy or a mystery story. A few years later, the gathering assembled in the living room around a television console, again for news and for Arthur Godfrey, or *Captain Video*, or a western story.

We kids were in perpetual motion: little Petie rocked on a fancy, handmade, ornately painted rocking horse and we twins rocked in twin rocking duck seats—presents from Santa. Later, we dressed in fine cowboy and cowgirl outfits and ran the long hallway, drawing shiny six-shooters and blasting away with the "bang-bang" of exploding caps. We also managed to get into mischief frequently. Once after the radio room had just been repapered, we found the bright walls a wonderful place to draw with our crayons. Mom went berserk—a favorite term of ours—and called over to the Lewises, a block away, asking cousin Deborah to come and watch us while Mom tried to clean the drawings off the wall before Pop showed up.

During our daily play, Grandma occasionally interrupted our games, sending us to the bottom of the steps to fetch the groceries that had been delivered. Back in the kitchen, we riffled through the paper sacks, looking for the white oleo in a clear plastic bag. A red dot of dye sat inside a bubble in the center of the covering. We kids vied to pop the dye bubble and mix it throughout the bag, turning the white oleo to a buttery-looking yellow. We helped out in the kitchen until we got too much underfoot and Grandma sent us out to play on the second-story porch or in the yard.

Grandma also let us go downstairs with her to Martin's dark green bakery truck, which stopped at our house on its way to the businesses uptown. We all climbed into the narrow, sweet-smelling aisle, eyeing all stainless steel trays filled with raisin cookies, lady fingers, berry tarts, pies, frosted cakes, and crusty bread. While Grandma selected rolls and desserts, Ted Veno, the swarthy deliveryman, handed us each a doughnut wrapped in waxed paper, quipping, "Start at the center and eat your way to the outside."

Occasionally, some places became off limits to us— such as anywhere Randall Yeagle was. Whenever this skinny, jittery plumber showed up, we children were put out of earshot. Jabbering incessantly, he got on Grandma's nerves with his constant yelling and cursing as he banged the old pipes. Once he left a job half-finished—with tools and pipes all about the bathroom sink—and didn't return for hours. When Grandma asked what took him so long, he shouted, "Why, Mrs. Wright, I had to go on the *Niña*, the *Pinta*, and the *Santa María* to find parts for this old plumbing."

Whatever the trend in children's clothes and toys, we little McClelland kids crested the first wave. For a brief time, beginning in May of 1946, Mom and our aunts ran a small children's store two doors away. We kids wore fancy outfits from the Tot Shop inventory, even months after it had closed. Continuing throughout our childhood and youth we always wore the smartest clothes, even when Mom had to carry credit balances on several store accounts to manage it.

Uncle Ben built us a roomy playhouse. Uncle Lloyd and Aunt Sally doted on us, frequently taking us on day trips. Everyone pitched in helping Mom put on lavish birthday parties with scads of schoolmates, decorations galore, twin cakes, scoops of rich ice cream, and an indulgence of gifts. As youngsters, we busy McClelland kids couldn't imagine anyone ever being lonely in that house. Yet, after putting us kids to bed, our mom spent endless nights inconsolably lonely.

Mom always enjoyed local events and relished an opportunity to take us kids on an outing. A Fourth of July celebration just after the soldiers returned home from the war turned out differently than planned. Although I was too young at the time to realize the turn of events, my brother helped me remember them quite some time later. Masontown's police department had long sponsored the PALS Club (Police Athletic League). As part of the postwar festivities, the PALS Club planned a Fourth of July fireworks display following a baseball game at the Sandy Bottom field. We kids sat in the stands with Mom, eating hot dogs and drinking orange soda, and then waiting and waiting for it to get dark. We could see a group of firemen setting up the display on the other side of the outfield fence. Finally, at dusk the men set off the first rockets. One of them flew straight up into the dark sky and quickly shot down again, landing directly in the center of the fireworks and spraying sparks everywhere. The firemen tore off in all directions, some bounding over the fence into the field of play, just as all of the fireworks ignited at once and shot off brilliantly in every direction. People all around us stood up, screaming and laughing. Some were awestruck at the loud inferno and some were pointing and laughing at the escaping firemen. Mom grabbed us twins by the hand and began dragging us out of the stands. Pete was tugging us in the opposite direction, trying to see all of the conflagration that he could. Mom screamed above the noise of the explosions and the crowd for him to let go and come to the car immediately. Inside the safety of the car we watched the last of the colorful smoke drift across the field as Mom drove us back home.

Sometime during our toddler years, amidst the hustle and bustle of that home, we kids became aware of not having a father. Of course, I have no memory of my realization. Was it at the Sunday dinner table? During a Christmas visit to my paternal grandparents' home at the edge of town? Had we overheard a conversation? Seen a picture? Or did our older cousins tell us? However our first and successive questions about Dad came about, they were met with curt answers. For years and years I was told only that my dad had been killed in the war against the Germans. Other than that, my family revealed nothing about the circumstances of his death at age twenty-nine, when I was just over a year old. Dinner table stories abounded about town characters, about friends like Mom's high school companion Phyllis Cowell, and about distant family members like Uncle Clarence. However, I heard next to nothing about my dad. When I did, it was happenstance.

For years Mom held us close to her, like the proverbial hen protectively gathering her chicks under outspread wings. Then she got a scare. When a mobile x-ray truck offered the opportunity for people to get checked for tuberculosis, Mom's x-ray looked suspicious. She was given her x-ray negative and told to check out a dark spot on her chest with her family physician. Mom was beside herself until she got in to see Dr. Peters. After he looked closely at the x-ray, he turned to Mom, smiling.

"What?" she insisted.

"Marianna, do you have a necklace with a cross on it?"

"Oh, Lord! Is that all it was?"

Even though the TB scare turned out to be a fluke, Mom decided that she had better loosen the apron strings and let us get used to being away from her, just in case something did happen to her. So, we began to spend weekends at various relatives' houses. When we were barely age-eligible for church camp, off we went. I remember, that first year, looking through the cabin's screen door and crying, as Mom—handkerchief to her face—drove away. Then, a scary idea hit us, touching off wild speculation. "What if we become orphans?" Mary Jane wondered aloud.

One afternoon, when Grandma discovered she needed a few more things for dinner, she placed a grocery order over the telephone and sent me uptown to pick it up at Howard's store. She told Paulie, the store-owner, to let me have a Hershey bar. I skipped up the block past our neighbors' houses under a darkening fall sky. Slowing to a walk at the edge of the business dis-trict, I was breathing hard, enjoying the crisp air. Sud-denly, I heard, "Hey, you're Pete McClelland's boy, ain't you?" A short, stocky man leaning on a parking meter seemed to be barking at me. It wasn't the thick accent, but the loud, gruff voice that scared me. He grinned at me glassy-eyed.

"I'm Watty Tassone. I mined with your dad. Which one are you?"

"Benny."

"Put 'er there, Benny." He reached for my hand. My uncle Lloyd had been instructing me in giving a good, firm handshake. *Put your hand in, like this, and hook your thumb over here. Now, squeeze. Harder. Now, pump up and down about three times. Not that high. Good and steady, like this. All right, try it again. Put your hand in, like this . . .* But I couldn't grip Watty's hand. It was too wide and the crusty hard fingers just wrapped around my whole hand. He grasped me and I tried not to let him see me wince. He pulled me close and grinned again.

Now I saw the teeth missing here and there, top and bottom. His breath was steamy sweet from the Trocadero Bar's boilermakers: shot of whiskey, beer chaser. He kept hold of me, grinning and staring unsteadily in my direction, like he was looking through me. I tried to move back to get some fresh air. Then his eyes focused again.

"Yeah, you favor him. We worked a four-foot vein one summer. He was damn near six feet tall. Swung the pickax and shoveled from his knees the whole shift. Worked harder than any man, Pete did. Why, once we mined forty tons in a single day. Nobody beat that. Never.

"He was a good man. You be proud, boy. Hold your head up high in this town." Turning wistful, he repeated slowly, "Yessir, he was a good man, Pete was."

He stared out over my head and loosened his grip. I slipped away and pushed Howard's door open, walking into the familiar smells of coffee, fresh produce, and sundry dry goods.

Years later, when Watty left mining, he grew and sold vegetables to occupy himself. He faithfully stopped at 201, and Mom faithfully bought something (mostly lima beans, as I recall). Whenever I was present, I never heard either of them say anything that would reveal that they shared a personal history with my dad. However, I want to believe that they shared a tacit understanding of younger, happier days when my dad was with them. These polite transactions went on until they both grew very old and his arthritis forced him out of gardening.

4

THE MEMORIAL DAY
PARADE AND CEREMONY

Masontown, Pennsylvania
May 1948

We watched the Memorial Day parade from our screened-in, second-story porch, shouting and waving to neighbors lining the street and to friends marching in the parade. The region's high school bands, Scout troops, and men in uniforms marched, carrying banners. New convertibles and old, shined-up roadsters puttered slowly by, bedecked with crepe paper, pretty girls, and dignitaries. Youngsters rode bicycles with red, white, and blue streamers trailing from the handlebars and woven between the spokes. Firemen clung to the sides and the back of their newest truck, as the driver revved up the engine, flashed its lights, and blew its horn and siren. Men and women in brightly colored western outfits rode well-groomed horses. One lady in a fancy suit and a top hat sat astride a high-stepping Tennessee walker that made a loud clop-clop-clop sound as it gaited by. Several children rode their ponies, some with braided manes and long ribbons intertwined in their tails.

Just after the American Legion contingent passed by our house, Mom led my older brother, my sister, and me through the side street, across Washington Street, and beyond the red stone parking lot by the football field to the cemetery. Mom carried a triangular-folded flag that she had taken from a box in her closet. The scent of mothballs swirled around us as we walked. When we neared the large trees by the cemetery's entrance, we could hear the combined church choirs singing "The Battle Hymn of the Republic."

In the beauty of the lilies Christ was born across the sea, / With a glory in His bosom that transfigures you and me: . . .

At the entrance, Mom paused, looked around slowly, took a deep breath, and waded into the crowd, nodding her head with a fixed smile as folks greeted her.

As He died to make men holy, let us die to make men free, / While God is marching on. / Glory! Glory! Hallelujah! / Glory! Glory! Hallelujah! / Glory, glory, Hallelujah! / His truth is marching on.

We made our way through the crowd of townsfolk to the reserved chairs at the front. The Breakwells, the Vittones, and the McCanns were already seated there, along with others I didn't know. Several women held folded flags on their laps. Grandmother McClelland, with her shiny pin of the Gold Star Mothers, had saved seats for us next to her.

In front of the choirs, on a row of chairs facing us sat lots of preachers. I knew our minister, Reverend Shields, and recognized my buddy Ronnie Smith's minister, Reverend Enid Pierce, as well as Father Kolb, the priest at the church my cousins Tommy Dick and Rosemary attended, and Father Gaydos from the Russian Orthodox church. The priests were dressed in black suits with stiff white collars around their necks. Reverend Shields wore a navy blue suit and a striped tie. Mrs. Pierce stood out in a light blue jacket and skirt with matching hat and shoes; a colorful, long, silk scarf draped down the front of her white blouse. Next to her sat some men in different kinds of service uniforms; they had medals like the ones I had seen in Mom's bottom dresser drawer. On the end in dark business suits sat men whom Mom called "our representatives." They offered prayers and made speeches between the hymns the choir sang. Grandma McClelland sang and hummed along with the choir. When they sang "My Country, 'Tis of Thee" and came to "land where my fathers died," I thought of what my family had said earlier during the parade: your father was a war hero, died for our country, saved the world from the Nazis.

As the ceremony progressed, the flag on Mom's lap, warmed by the sun, radiated waves of mothball odor, as did the uniforms of the solemn-faced men who marched crisply past us in single file, rifles shouldered, to the woods where the gravestones ended. Following muted commands, piercing rifle shots flew into the blinding sun overhead. A pair of startled birds flapped out of the trees. After a pause came another volley. Another pause and another volley. Just when I recovered from one sound blast, another one hit. With each rifle report Mom's head jerked. She had to straighten her hat. She dabbed a white handkerchief with embroidered eyelets at the tears streaming down her reddened face. At some point I buried my head in the flag on her lap, breathing in mothball air. When the firing stopped and the soldiers filed back again, I turned my head up and squinted, trying to see who they were. I knew they were dads who hadn't died.

During the long silence that followed, I began looking around to see if another speaker was going to step forward, but none did. Finally, a beautiful, sad sound came from over in the older part of the cemetery. It was a horn. A trumpet, somebody called it. They said it was one of the DeBolt boys playing "Taps" by his granddaddy's grave, one made after the First World War.

As the church choirs began singing "Onward, Christian Soldiers," Mom suddenly motioned for us to leave.

Like a mighty army moves the church of God; . . .

As we passed by the Breakwells, the Vittones, the McCanns, and others, women reached out and touched Mom's arm.

This through countless ages man and angels sing. / Onward, Christian soldiers, marching as to war, . . .

As schoolkids, we marched in Memorial Day parades year after year, carrying banners with our classmates or wearing uniforms with our Scout troop. My brother might even have marched in the school band during a hapless time when he tried to play the French horn. Some say Pete could have managed even such a difficult instrument, except that he couldn't stomach the tantrums of the aging band director. Just the mention of the name "Vito" sent Pete into a torrent of expletives, as he pictured the imperious, balding man with puffy, dark circles under his eyes, breaking his baton in disgust on the podium, bulldog jowls shaking, as he screamed at the "idiots" before him.

Mom, however, stayed put during successive Memorial Days. With the horns blaring and the drums pounding as the bands marched under her bedroom window, Mom lay prostrate on her bed, comforted by a box of Kleenex.

5

THE WAR HONOR ROLL

Masontown, Pennsylvania
September 1949

Surely we had walked past the War Honor Roll before, my twin sister and I, but I hadn't paid attention to it. Set on the southwest corner of our schoolyard, facing the intersection of Washington and Church streets, the monument was erected out of the same yellow brick as our school building. A wide paved walkway led several yards from the corner of the sidewalk up to the monument and the flagpole. Our church stood directly across the street; our home on Main Street was just two blocks away.

Jackie Belch, Ronnie Smith, Johnny Schultz, and I were neighborhood pals throughout all the elementary and junior high grades. In summer we played cowboys and Indians in Neff's Woods. Through the years we worked together on endless Cub Scout and Boy Scout projects and camped in the mountains. The vagaries of high school, such as dating and playing sports, separated us but never broke the bonds. Often we had spats. Maybe someone would run home mad. But we always patched things up. Each fall we wrestled to decide who was top dog. Ronnie, the smallest, had three older brothers and a fierce need not to be dominated. He won every time, even when it meant drawing blood, which it often did.

At recess we four first-graders played tag, running the width of the schoolyard. The flagpole was "home." One time, when Ronnie was "it" and I clung to the safety of the silver pole, he sneaked around the front of the monument, trying to catch me off guard. Johnny and Jackie ran in short circles around the monument, coming nearer and nearer, tempting Ronnie with the singsong chant "Nah, nahuh, na-huh. You ca-an't get me!" That's when he said it.

"Hey, Benny, come here! Your name's on here."

"Can't fool me, Ronnie. You're 'it' and I'm staying on 'home.'"

"Betcha a dime, it's here. Look," he spelled, "M-c-C-l-e-l-l-a-n-d."

"You better not be lyin'. Time out." We all walked around to the front and peered through the glass at twelve columns of names, gold letters pressed into wood. There it was, midway down the center column: Ewing R. McClelland. I didn't act surprised.

"Oh," I said as casually as I could. "It's my dad." Again, words my family had repeated flew into my head: war hero, died in the world war, saved us from Hitler and the Nazis. I sucked in some air.

"How come that star's there?"

The sun glinted off a five-corner star to the left of his name.

"Uh."

"'Cause he got killed," Johnny put in. "See, there's one here by Mrs. Kratz's husband and John Vittone's uncle."

"Shut up!" I turned away, smelling those mothballs from an opened box in Mom's closet.

Reentering the classroom, I saw our teacher, Mrs. Seckler, printing spelling words on the board. What a relief I felt, grasping the thick, dark green pencil, checking the point, and beginning to copy the words in my notepad. I could lose myself studying for the next test.

Clara Lee Seckler, a thirty-something mother of four girls, was a tall, elegant woman of fine manners, bright eyes, a slender nose, and wavy blonde hair. She had grown up on a farm adjacent to the Frosts, my paternal grandmother's family. She and Mom were close friends and taught across the hall from each other. Mary Jane and I liked going to school. We fit in there as easily as at home and church. Mary Jane mixed better than I did socially; I worked harder for recognition from adults. She enjoyed wide popularity; I stayed within a small circle. She might get caught dallying and giggling with some other girls in the cloakroom; I liked to pull pranks, but I tried to make sure I wouldn't get caught. And I liked doing teacher's pet jobs, like erasing the board and dusting the erasers outside on the school wall. Usually, I did this after school, while we waited for Mom to get things ready for the next day and clear her desk.

All through grade school I played in that schoolyard. The War Honor Roll, always there, came and went in my consciousness. I never knew and heard little about my father, but I sometimes felt him palpably in my life. As a fifth-grade patrol boy, I was posted at the Washington and Church streets intersection daily. We raised the flag in the morning and lowered it at the end of the day. I had known years earlier how the flag was supposed to be folded into a triangle. After a while I never had to look at the War Honor Roll. Day after day I could just feel it there with that gold star blazing in the sun. And in my mind.

Like that gold star and the smell of mothballs, a pair of parentheses was also an enduring emblem of my dilemma, my search to understand who I was a part of. Throughout my life, whenever parental information was required on school forms, I had to print "(deceased)" next to my dad's name. I felt that he stayed inside those parentheses and I was held on the outside, unable to see in. Beginning in those early years and continuing, off and on for over fifty years, I have been trying to learn more about my dad and his death and to understand what he and it meant to me. For so long I flew solo, traveling for years in this search process without realizing that many other veterans' children were also seeking paths into their fathers' pasts in order to discover their identities as well.

6

TALKING LIKE CROCKY

Masontown, Pennsylvania
June 1953

At the end of my fourth-grade year, Mom gave up teaching to take a new job as postmaster. The evening she came home from her first day at work, I was waiting atop the twenty-second step, the head of the stairs. From the window in her bedroom I had watched Mom park her dark blue 1950 Plymouth, a four-door sedan. Then I ran to the steps and perched behind the woven, wrought-iron gate. I had been folding and refolding my new yellow-and-green, plastic Valvoline cap, the one shaped like a soldier's cloth cap. The red grease rag still draped out of my back pants pocket, trailing the odor of dirty oil and grime from the handles of wrenches, hammers, and screwdrivers. When Mom opened the front door, I could finally show her what I had learned that day, my first day at work with the mechanics at the repair shop downstairs.

"Hi, Mom, you old bastard, you!" I shouted, beaming with pride.

She had reached the third step when that new word caromed off the horsehair plaster walls, dropping like a nine-ball into her ear. She grasped the iron railing, glared up at me in shock, mouth agape.

"What! What did you call me?" Her light-brown curls shook as she barked out each word.

"'You old bastard!'" I repeated, holding my courageous pose, even when her wailing, howling scream reached me as she clambered up the stairs.

"Just what is the big idea of using such language, young man!" she demanded, now red-faced, huffing and puffing, double-time, up the last few steps. "We do not use that kind of language in this house, I'll have you know!"

"You talk the way you want. I'm talking like Crocky Morris," I said, swaggering in the power of this new language, which had held sway all day among the men in the repair shop.

"We'll see about that. I'm calling Uncle Lloyd and we're going to have a talk, Mister Smart Aleck. He'll wash your mouth out with soap. Go to your room!" While she didn't mind giving us a whack or two to get us to settle down, for serious disciplinary matters Mom relied on male authority. In the absence of a husband, she called on her father or one of her brothers to have a man-to-man talk with us.

Under her fierce glare, I wilted and shuffled to my room, bewildered, wondering why she didn't share my joy of discovering a new world. I had just been introduced to a man's world where cussing a blue streak was not only a normal occurrence, but also a sign of one's savvy and put-down ability. By using the right combination of "SOBs," "chickenshits," and "jackasses," along with a selection of "numbskulls," "dimwits," and "morons," a man placed himself in a superior position to another man or relieved his frustration at an oil-pan bolt that wouldn't break loose or a tool that couldn't be found.

To be honest, not everyone in the repair shop swore. Jimmy was a soft-spoken, thirty-something, three-hundred pounder, with a cherubic round face, bugeyes, and bulging double chins. While he lost his temper frequently, he seethed more often than he blew up and, if he cussed, it was always under his breath, barely audible. The oldest of the men, Dan, kept a watchful eye on us boys. In his late fifties and peering through thick glasses, Dan was a short, slight, energetic hothead who often sent tools clanging across the floor in frustration. Dan usually unleashed a stream of epithets on his independent-thinking son, Danny, who had just finished high school. The younger man, who stood a foot taller than his dad and shared his short fuse, frequently spat back blasphemous profanity, using the Lord's name in vain and interjecting forms of the "f" and "mf" words at every opportunity. Sometimes father and son stood toe to toe, shouting, and more than once they came to blows. Keeping his distance from the rest, Bill stood stiffly erect. With creases pressed deeply into his pasty-white forehead and with naturally wavy brown hair impeccably combed back, continental style, Bill looked more like a salesman than a mechanic as he smoked unfiltered Camels, thoughtfully, methodically. When he drank, he did so discreetly after work at the fire hall. Although he may have sworn like the rest, in front of me

Bill kept his language as neat and clean as his uniform. Once Mom told my brother, Pete, that she had dated Bill at the same time that Dad and she began dating; in fact, she chose our dad over Bill when she decided to become serious. So, Pete found it humorous to watch Mom and Bill whenever she walked through the shop. It was, Pete reported, the briefest of formal exchanges. With the barest acknowledgment, they greeted each other:

"Marianna."

"Bill."

Crocky Morris, a wiry, little guy, was the parts man, gas pump attendant, and undisputed king of invective. With his mouth going a mile a minute, Crocky was a gadfly and a prankster. Stories of his endeavors abounded, like the one about his breaking in Mr. Diefenbecker's new car. In the years between the Great Depression and the Second World War, the automobile industry had made great advances in its products since the day of the Model Ts and the Model As. It was still decades before precision engineering, however, and cars needed to be "broken in" before they ran smoothly. A new-car owner could expect some minor engine problems for the first few hundred miles: the internal parts were stiff and the combustion components frequently needed fine-tuning. A long-time businessman with impeccable taste and fine manners, Mr. D. declined into effeteness in his middle age. He asked Crocky to drive the sedan for a while to break it in. Returning to the dealership in the middle of the next week, Mr. D. looked around for Crocky and finally inquired as to his whereabouts. No one in the shop seemed to know. In fact, they claimed that Crocky hadn't shown up for work since late last week. Placing several frantic phone calls from the sales office proved fruitless in locating the missing Mr. Morris. A week later, a tan-faced Crocky returned with Mr. D.'s sedan, quite well broken in and showing close to two thousand miles on the odometer. Crocky had seized the opportunity to tour a girlfriend through the South to Florida and back. He handed the car keys to an apoplectic Mr. D. and strolled away, chuckling to his buddies about what fine weather and good food he had found south of the Mason-Dixon Line.

I was enamored of Crocky's feisty charm and brash irreverence that first day that I followed my brother to his summer job. Pete, who was two years older, had already been working for Uncle Tom in the car dealership repair shop. He even had a time card on which to punch his check-in and check-out times at the big clock on the shop desk. He showed me the columns of numbers in blue ink on the green-lined card. Two years later I would join him in the work force and get a card, too, receiving ten cents an hour for running errands, sweeping the floor, and serving as general factotum in the shop. It would be a few more years before we could move the cars in and out of the shop, parking them in a diagonal pattern on the sales lot in the morning and squeezing them into tight spots in the repair shop at night. Pete and I might occasionally get a wash job when nobody else was available. Doing a good job brought hefty tips; a few quarters went a long way in a world where a Coke cost five cents and where you could buy a hamburger and a milkshake for fifty cents uptown at Ralston's.

Usually, however, washing and waxing cars was a specialty job handled by various short-term workers. Joe, a milkman, showed up some afternoons when he'd finished his route. Short and chubby, with an acne-scarred, ruddy complexion, Joe was a thoroughly ordinary-looking guy, except for his wavy, blondish-red hair, which glistened with Vitalis. When I first met him, he walked into the corner of the car wash space and said, "Look here," tilting his head for me to follow him. Opening his wallet, he handed me some explicit, black-and-white snapshots that revealed what occupied him on other afternoons with sundry women on his route. Seated on a blanket outdoors, a tall, amply endowed, blonde woman—pleasantly tanned, it appeared—looked right into the camera with an easy smile on her sensible-looking, oval-shaped face. The flawless beauty of the nude in the picture was marred only by a large, white gauze bandage wrapped around her left upper arm.

"What happened?" I asked, pointing to her arm.

"Oh, she burned herself. Steam from a spaghetti pot at supper the night before."

It jarred me, the incongruity. At first flushed with desire, I was now wrenched into trying to convert the image of this naked goddess into a clothed housewife, balancing a pot of boiling water over a colander in a kitchen sink.

Two other pictures were of a much younger, less mature girl—small, dark-haired, beautiful, and seated on a single bed. In the first picture, fully dressed in a white blouse and a long, dark, pleated skirt spread out, she looked skittishly into the camera with her face turned slightly away. In the next snapshot she had pulled the skirt completely over her head, exposing her naked lower body, spread-legged on the floral coverlet. Unlike the seductive charm of the first picture, this one emitted raw dirtiness. Had I known the word, pornography would have been on the tip of my tongue. When I told Pete about Joe's pictures, he explained that one of Joe's women had saved his life.

"Early one morning when he headed down a hill in the heavily loaded milk truck, the drive shaft snapped and dug into the roadbed, pole-vaulting the truck onto its roof and trapping Joe inside—knocked out cold, cut up by broken bottles, and nearly drowning in milk. This woman happened by on her way to work. Somehow she fished him out of the windshield space and wrapped him up until help came. When he healed up, they started to make out."

After hearing that, I shook my head at the curious way of the world. How could a woman ever look twice at Joe! He had some enigmatic appeal—something beyond looks, that's for sure.

The parts room was a world unto itself—the first "system" that I recall learning. I remember the sense of accomplishment when I learned how to navigate my way through the voluminous catalog to find a part for one of the mechanics. Spanning four feet across the front counter, a green metal book casing held the parts catalogs. First, I'd find the right book for the year, make, and model of car. Then, I'd flip through to locate the appropriate section—carburetor, brakes, electrical, engine, exhaust, ignition, transmission, suspension, etc. Then, I'd write down the item number. If we carried it in stock, I'd search through the bins to find the item number and retrieve the part. If it was a common seal, pump, brake shoe, or something else that was available locally, I'd dial the auto parts store, confirm that they had it, find out its price, get some petty cash, walk uptown to the store, pick up the part, and deliver it to the shop, putting the change in the drawer and attaching the receipt to the work order. Of course, Pete knew mechanics better than I and he understood our quirky system of stocking parts, so he could do the job faster, but I felt that I'd joined some special group once I mastered this job, too.

I also liked pumping gas. Even today, though I try to avoid inhaling the poisonous fumes at the pump, I inevitably recall those days when I pumped twenty-five-cents-a-gallon gas and enjoyed the sweet-smelling fumes, which always made Crocky sneeze. I liked everything about being the gas attendant: operating the hand crank to set the pump to zeros, squeezing the hose trigger to pump the gas, cleaning the windshield, checking the oil, gauging the tires, collecting the money, and making change. I especially liked to watch the gasoline deliveryman arrive in his tanker truck and fill up our underground tanks. It seemed a marvel of ingenuity when he dipped the long wooden measuring stick down into the ground to see how much gas was in the tanks.

The only people I didn't like to wait on were the preachers and priests. It wasn't anything against religion or against them personally, but the clergy received a 5 percent discount and they charged every purchase. That meant that I had to write up a sales slip, including doing the math by hand: multiplying the subtotal by .05 and subtracting that sum from the subtotal to come up with the total. It took so much time. Most folks were nice, but not Father Kolb. The Very Reverend Francis J. Kolb was an old, white-headed German-born priest, who, they said, was mean even to Catholics. I heard of a meek Italian-American schoolgirl, one of the nuns' pets, who was sent to buy chalk and paper for her class. She had to get money from Father Kolb, go to the store, make the purchases, and return to Father Kolb with a receipt and the change. She was shaking so badly before him that she dropped a dime in his office. He made her kneel on a round curtain rod for punishment. Father Kolb's sister bought him a big black De Soto or Chrysler every year or two. He was very particular about keeping it clean. I had to make certain not to let a drop of gas get on the finish. And at the desk he looked over my shoulder as I wrote each number in my calculations. He made me a nervous wreck. Often, I had to start over, because he distracted me so that I lost my place. I always wondered why the clergy got a discount at our place. The only thing I could imagine was that Grandma Wright had something to do with it, since her father had been a minister Up East and her mother, Gram, was so big in the church at Ronco.

Over time I discovered a world of experiences working in the family business, but that first day in the shop I worshipped the Tower of Babel, Crocky Morris. With his cunning use of vituperative words, Crocky was my hero. By the end of that first day, however, a man of real authority, of clear unimpeachable rectitude, set the record straight in short order. Uncle Lloyd was an especially generous man, who took us kids on road adventures and bought us neat gifts, like Mickey Mouse watches, flash cameras, and footlockers. Each Christmastime throughout our childhood, he took a picture of us in some creative pose, developed it, and printed several holiday greeting cards for us to send. We loved going to his and Aunt Sally's house across the river in Waynesburg, because they joyously opened their doors wide to us. They always stocked a supply of toys, games, and the latest gizmos. They put on sumptuous backyard barbecues. And if Mom and we kids popped in unannounced, they would whip up a great meal in a moment's notice. Perhaps they enjoyed us all the more since they had no children.

However, when it came to the matter of discipline—whether as school principal or uncle—Uncle Lloyd brooked no nonsense and resolutely carried out swift and sure justice. While threats of both a paddle and a bar of soap were made during the Crocky Morris incident, I don't recall if I suffered either. What I do recall are Uncle Lloyd's stern words and pointed index finger that gave me an understanding—"in no uncertain terms, young man"—that we were different from the men who worked in the shop.

"Yes, we associate with them, even work right alongside them. But we are different. And one thing that is different, for certain, is that we speak politely. We do not use such language."

When I weakly protested that I had heard Pop say "SOB" once, I quickly regretted opening my mouth, because it lengthened and intensified the lecture I was receiving. I was told that Pop might have said that in a story, when he was using somebody else's words, but he did not talk like that and neither could I. "Do you understand me, Young Mister Benjamin?" Indeed, I understood that I had better not use Crocky's language within earshot of my family—nor should I acknowledge having overheard Pop using it.

Working at the family business off and on into our teens, my brother, Pete, and I learned a lot about the world of men even if it took a little extra instruction at first for me to reckon where our family fit in it—and to understand the double standard by which some adults lived. I often wondered how different my introduction to male culture might have been had my dad lived to be head of our household. At one time I thought that I would have grown up in a more rural scene, among miners and farmers. However, when I learned that my dad had been studying to be an optometrist before he enlisted in the army, I fantasized what life would have been like growing up in a new suburb among families of other professionals. But fate carried me from Grandma Wright's kitchen to the repair shop where Crocky, Danny, and Joe served unwittingly as some of my first mentors.

1

FAMILY HERITAGE PERSONIFIED

Masontown, Pennsylvania
Throughout the 1900s

Mom helped us kids shape our early perceptions of our relatives. For instance, she considered Aunt Sally an ancestor worshipper. Aunt Sally was fond of telling about her family line that led back to John Minor, who established Greene County—where Aunt Sally lived all of her life—naming it after the Revolutionary War great, General Nathaniel Greene. While Uncle Lloyd, Mom's oldest brother, shared this keen passion for genealogy with his wife, Mom wouldn't think of criticizing him. She deeply respected him and thought that his love of lineage didn't seem so racially engrossed as our aunt's did. Uncle Lloyd and Aunt Sally, both lifelong educators, loved us youngsters and followed our progress throughout our school years and adulthood, cheering for our successes and suffering over our failures—though never uncritically about either. We felt their powerful influence and the weight of their judgment at every juncture of our lives. For them above all others, we knew that we had a family tradition of which we should ever be mindful.

Sometime in the sixties, Uncle Lloyd gave as Christmas gifts to each of his siblings a white ceramic plaque with a colorful Wright Family Coat of Arms. He had mounted each plaque on red velvet and framed it in golden oak. On the back of each frame he glued a copy of a brief genealogical history, "The Wright Family And Its Coat of Arms." Then, decades later and just a few years before his death, Uncle Lloyd traced our family lineage, handwriting a ten-page letter in his attractive and still-steady calligrapher's script. Referring to "The Wright Family And Its Coat of Arms," he wrote, "From this you will see that one Wm Wright was among the passengers of the 'Mayflower' when it arrived at Plymouth in 1620. Samuel, Richard, Benjamin, Anthony and Thomas Wright are recorded to have come a few years later, but it is not known as to what connection they had with the original settler. (This you can read on this paper.) But my reason for mentioning it is the familiar family names—William (my Uncle Will), Richard (my father), Benjamin (my grandfather and brother), and Thomas (my uncle, brother and his son and grandson). This is characteristic with families and oft times makes it difficult, but is also a good sign of family ties."

Proud as he was of this possible distant connection to a passenger on the *Mayflower*, Uncle Lloyd was prouder, and more certain, of his relation to the dozens of family members from the mid-1840s to the mid-1980s whom he listed in this long epistle, carefully annotating birth dates, birth places, spouses, children, and dates of death for those deceased. "What I give you here," he noted, "is what I know to be. I have met all of these folks mentioned except my Grandfather Lloyd and Grandmother Keating, but lived with both of their spouses." Understandably, for a man whose world had been rocked by two world wars, by the depression, by

Nixon's disgrace, and by the social upheaval of the sixties, this certain knowledge of one's place in the family of human beings was a sustaining force, just as were his memberships in exclusive fraternal societies, with their historical and quasi-sacred rites.

Born Lloyd Austin Wright in 1906 in nearby Edenborn, German Township, Mom's oldest brother was nine years her senior. Pop had paved the way for him to excel and Uncle Lloyd masterfully assumed his position as a leader. He came of age during the period of unparalleled growth in Pop's business ventures and untrammeled ascendancy in his civic and political activities. In the years prior to the Great Depression ours was a prosperous and influential family. Decades after the economic disaster, family members referred fondly to the boom times when they traveled frequently in a Lincoln touring car, which had built-in wooden suitcases crafted by furniture makers. A frequent destination was Up East, our family's term for the region around Scranton and Wilkes-Barre, the hard-coal fields where both sides of the family had their beginning in this country. Uncle Lloyd revered his forebears, fondly recalling some of his earliest memories of traveling Up East with Gram.

If Pop was the head of the household in which Uncle Lloyd grew up, still there was a matriarch with whom everyone had to reckon: born in Wales on October 1, 1852, Mary Ann Williams was Uncle Lloyd's maternal grandmother, lovingly called Gram. She lived in the Wright family home when Mom and her siblings were being raised. Because she died before I was born, I had a hard time placing Gram in time when I heard stories about her. Where did she fit in the olden days? Learning about a memorable childhood event that she experienced while on holiday in London helped me answer the question. When she was just twelve years old, Gram and her family were vacationing in London when she heard that the American president had been assassinated. His name, she learned, was Abraham Lincoln.

Gram married a young navy officer and bore him a son. When both the husband and son died in an epidemic of fever, Gram moved back home with her father and her sister. A stonemason and president of the local bank, the father supported them well, until the bank failed, causing them to move on in search of a better life. First, they tried London and later moved to the United States. After coming to the States, Gram got married again, this time to Ebenezer Lloyd, a Welsh miner and a minister several years her senior, who lived in Exeter, Pennsylvania. Although Presbyterian, Ebenezer pastored at a Baptist church in Dorrancetown. The Lloyds had a son, Ebenezer, who died in infancy. Then came three daughters, including Deborah, who was Uncle Lloyd and Mom's mother, my grandma.

Calamity struck again when Ebenezer Lloyd died. Judging from the large formal photographic portrait, which still hung in Gram's former bedroom when I was a youngster, Ebenezer Lloyd was an intense-looking man: broad forehead, deep- and close-set dark eyes, classic oval-shaped face accented by a mustache and a full chin beard. Next to the portrait hung a tribute to him designed by a devoted parishioner, whose name I never learned. A small print of Ebenezer's portrait in the center of the page was flanked on the left by a Welsh version of the tribute and on the right by an English version. Written poetically, the tribute consisted of seven eight-line stanzas with alternately rhyming lines that listed his many virtues and apotheosized him. It concluded with a note of concern for Gram and the girls:

> *May the dark cloud soon be brightened*
> *For the widow left alone;*

May His sun shine on the orphans
Till they meet in yonder home.

Following Ebenezer's death, Gram moved with her three daughters—Claude, Deborah, and Lydia—to Ronco in southwestern Pennsylvania, where new coal mines were being dug. There she opened a boarding-house for miners. She soon became a commanding public presence, founding the Union Church with families from various—mostly Protestant—faiths. She served as its Sunday school superintendent, and she established a chapter of the Woman's Christian Temperance Union. She was also in demand in the region as a capable attending nurse at births. She coached the church's girls' basketball team, with her three daughters as its major players. For uniforms, Gram made long, navy blue skirts and matching cloaks with red lining in the hoods. Grandma, the middle child, often talked about the fierce competition that they faced in some of the rough areas. If they won an away game, she recalled, it could be more dangerous walking outside than it had been running on the court.

Gram must have found inspiration from such con-temporaries as Susan B. Anthony and Elizabeth Cady

Stanton. Carrying out her work on behalf of women and children in the male-dominated coal fields, this outspoken Welsh woman not only gave men a piece of her mind on gender politics and abstinence from alcohol, but she also practiced what she preached, expecting to be taken seriously—as seriously as a man would be.

The Lloyd daughters helped with the chores around the boardinghouse. Grandma told us that her first job was to trim the oil lamp wicks, clean the chimneys, and fill the lamps with oil. With the girls helping her, Gram served a large Sunday dinner at noon, with two meats and an array of vegetable dishes. For the light Sunday evening meal, they put out cold cuts, hard-boiled eggs, cheese, and bread. Once, when helping set up the Sunday evening buffet, the girls blew the insides out of several eggs and placed the shells on top of the egg plate. They hid behind the curtains and laughed as the miners reached for the eggs, crushing the empty shells in their hands. Gram gave them a sound talking to, ending with her dire warning: "John Thomas will get you if you don't behave." Still I wonder if she didn't have a good laugh over the prank privately, as it was reported that she enjoyed playing a practical joke as well. For example, we often heard about the time she invited a visiting minister for Sunday dinner. Seated next to him at the table, Gram stirred her tea with her spoon and then furtively laid the hot silver on his hand, guffawing when he nearly jumped out of his seat. Her admixture of rectitude and tricksterism came through in a variety of forms in Gram's descendants—and Uncle Lloyd was a prime example.

Even though he was proud that his initials spelled "LAW," Uncle Lloyd had elbowroom to explore youthful adventures. Most of these peccadilloes involved cars and speed, but the common theme is Uncle Lloyd's impatience to get somewhere in a hurry, rather than his being a speed demon. One such incident involved his flaunting the law and fleeing a vindictive lawman, as my brother reminded me with this story. Uncle Lloyd drove a Model T Ford as soon as he was tall enough to reach the controls. One time when driving (underage) back home from Ronco, he was stopped just outside of town by a state highway patrolman on horseback. Intent on punishing Uncle Lloyd on the spot, the patrolman told him to stand out on the running board. When he did, the patrolman began beating him with his quirt, whereupon Uncle Lloyd jumped back in the car and sped on his way as fast as he could to Pop's establishment. The patrolman chased him, the horse's hooves pounding away on the hard pavement. Pulling around to the back lot, Uncle Lloyd jumped out of the car, ran into the shop, climbed into the center hole of a stack of tires, and hid. Galloping into the front lot, the patrolman couldn't see Lloyd or the car. Dismounting, he went into the shop and, gasping, demanded to know the whereabouts of "that Wright boy." Nobody, it appeared, knew. The patrolman vowed to catch up with him, threatening emptily, "And when I do . . ."

In another incident with the law, so the family story goes, Uncle Lloyd was driving uptown, approaching the major intersection of Main and Church streets. In an attempt to keep an orderly flow of traffic through the bottleneck, the town officials had erected a wooden stanchion in the center of the road. Drivers were to keep to the right, or outside, of the post. Uncle Lloyd decided that he could get past some cars stopped ahead of him by cutting on the inside of the post as he turned left. A policeman stopped him, shouting for him to turn that car back to the outside of the post. When Uncle Lloyd began talking back to him about their damn post causing a worse backup of traffic, the officer reached into the car and wrenched the wooden steering wheel, accidentally breaking it off. Getting out of the car, Uncle Lloyd handed the wheel to the cop, saying, "Here. You take this to my dad. Tell him who broke it and that he can find his car uptown where you left it." Uncle Lloyd walked the two blocks home. In a meeting to discuss the altercation, Pop offered to pay a fine for his son's moving traffic violation only if the city agreed to pay for a new steering wheel and a towing charge. No charges were filed.

Once, Uncle Lloyd's youthful impatience brought him up short. In a hurry to get on the road in a car with wooden spokes, he failed to check whether the wood needed to be wet down with the water hose. Dry spokes shrank and loosened from the axle and rim holes. He hopped in the tin lizzie and roared out to the end of the alley, turning quickly onto Washington Street. As it rounded the curve, the car flew off all four wheels, its axles sliding to a halt on the brick pavement and wheel spokes splintering and flying in all directions. Disgusted with the lost time, he had only to walk a block to the shop to fetch some help. No doubt he heard a fatherly lecture on the theme of a stitch in time.

If privileged as a youngster and if occasionally indulged by a proud father, Uncle Lloyd had earned

Pop's respect by being an industrious young man with sound values and a tireless diligence to complete whatever task he undertook. Like his father, he was skilled in every sort of manual labor, he liked gadgets, he was bright in business affairs, and he was popular among his peers. Underage or not, he would put in a full day's work with the other men in his father's business. When new cars arrived by rail on a flatcar at Pittsburgh, young Lloyd joined the crew that picked them up and drove them back to his dad's dealership. The new vehicles had been stacked on the flatcar like elephants in a circus act finale, standing on hind legs with front feet up on another pachyderm's back. After railroad workmen unpacked the load and signed the release papers, the Wright crew went to work, putting on the wheels, adjusting the brakes, and gassing them up. This was often dangerous work, as the men were always working against time. Once Uncle Lloyd's cousin—who was also a youngster—was working under the front end of a car and someone drove over his leg, breaking his ankle.

When they set out driving south, they formed a tight caravan of six cars—this, too, like circus elephants parading with tails and trunks intertwined—because they had licenses on only the lead and last cars. Wending their way through steel towns along the river, over

the ridges of the Allegheny Mountains and across low-
land farming communities, the drivers would pull into
town by dusk, barring any major mishaps. Of course,
some maintenance was considered routine on a long
drive then, such as changing a few tires, making further
brake adjustments, and stopping at mountain springs
to fill up overheated radiators.

Graduating in 1925 from German Township High
School, Uncle Lloyd completed his baccalaureate study
across the river in Greene County, at Waynesburg College in 1929. While at college, he also found time to have
fun, joining Delta Sigma Phi and eventually becoming
its president. Always a smart dresser, Uncle Lloyd found
an equally sharp partner in Sarah McKay, a local high-
school girl, who also matched him in wit and social
charm. One weekend, so the family story went, Uncle
Lloyd came home, dressed up in his best duds, took a
new Ford out of the showroom and set off to Waynesburg to pick up the divine Miss M. A little behind
schedule, he cruised at top speed, until he failed to
negotiate a curve and wrecked the car. He hitched a ride
home, told Pop where he had wrecked, made a long-distance phone call to say that he'd be later than expected,
selected another new car from the showroom, and went

on his way, driving only a little bit slower this time. Depending on who was recounting this incident, he might add, "And brother Tom was mad as a hornet, thinking that Lloyd was the apple of his father's eye."

After college, instead of going into business with his father, Uncle Lloyd devoted himself to education, returning to his high school as a teacher. He married his college sweetheart, Sarah McKay, who also chose a teaching career. The Great Depression, which hit at about this time, had a powerful impact on Uncle Lloyd. Fifty years later he referred to it using the phrase "through which many of my years were spent." In fact, he had lived over twenty years before that decade and fifty afterwards at the time of his recollection, but the devastating economic and psychological trauma of those days made the depression era seem a much longer period of time than it was.

Over the next decade, Uncle Lloyd taught at nearby German Township High School, eventually stepping up as the school's principal, a job he held for thirty years until his retirement in 1971. His name became synonymous with the school. He did everything from taking and developing pictures for the yearbooks to coaching forensics—leading several award-winning teams, including state champions. He was instrumental in forging new school sports associations and in forming new school districts in the region, when consolidation made good educational and economic sense.

He was a man's man in a male-ordered world. Following his college fraternity membership, he devoted his out-of-school time to the Masonic Lodge. He served as Past Master of the Valley Lodge, Masontown, 1945, and was a member of the Uniontown Lodge of Perfection, Consistory of Pittsburgh, Thirty-Second Degree, Syria Temple. Except for his position as principal, he didn't enter the same public political arena his father had. However, very much his father's son in his confident demeanor and assertive leadership abilities, Uncle Lloyd handled the political demands of his job and his fraternal organizations with aplomb. A forceful public speaker and a great storyteller, he seemed most himself when he was instructing someone, whether it was in carpentry or in memory work for a secret Masonic ceremony. Though he tried several times to join the armed services, a hernia forced him to remain a civilian, something that was hard for him to accept, especially when his younger brothers, many of his friends, and my dad went off to war.

Uncle Lloyd faithfully sent us kids his thoughts in letters, notes, and cards. He was constant in this practice when I was growing up and saw him almost daily, as well as when I left home after high school. He may have picked up the habit as a youngster, traveling with Gram. Looking through family memorabilia, I found boxes of pictures from the photo-snapping family, but the amount of correspondence—of all varieties—outnumbered everything else. And Gram's letters sent to her daughter with detailed news from the family Up East numbered among the earliest documents. Surveying this considerable collection, I realized that those in our earlier generations were correspondents. Everyone sent each other cards, mailed news clippings, and left long notes when leaving home. During the Second World War, the development of V-mail technology fascinated our family members, enabling them to write a full-page letter which was reduced by a photocopier to half-sheet size, and then airmailed. Of course, I recall that when we kids received a card or note from someone in the family, money always fell out when we opened it. Oh, what a godsend a few dollars out of the blue were back then!

We kids were also trained early to write. Late in his life Uncle Lloyd came upon—and sent back to me—a note that I had written him from the cabin at the Lake o' the Woods as soon as I could write cursive. When we kids went off to camp each summer, Mom sent with each of us a stack of stamped postcards preaddressed to her and to each of our relatives. She instructed us to send one every day. As much a mom as a postmaster, she had posted letters to us days before we left for camp, so that on our first full day there we received mail. Needless to say, we were more embarrassed than grateful, being the only campers to get mail on the first day. As adults, Mary Jane and Pete have remained the most faithful correspondents among us McClelland kids. When Pete and I moved far away from the family in Masontown to study or work, we recorded audio-tape letters and mailed them to one another. Now that e-mail is convenient, we use it. As in love with gadgets and as eager to communicate as he was, Uncle Lloyd would no doubt be the biggest cyberbug among us, if he were with us today. However, no e-mail message could excite us nearly as much as seeing Uncle Lloyd's distinctive script on an arriving envelope did.

In his retirement years Uncle Lloyd continued an active life, occupying himself with numerous hobbies and self-appointed tasks. He helped with the upkeep of 201, where Mom continued to live alone. He also helped my brother Pete on his Turkey Hollow farm outside Waynesburg. At various times there were chicken, cattle, and sheep on the farm. Pete told me that when Uncle Lloyd arrived in the morning, he walked into the kitchen, removed the tall cap from a bottle of Irish whiskey, filled it, and drank the liquor in a swallow. Clearing his throat, he quipped, "Why feel like a bum all day, when for fifty cents you can feel like a millionaire!" The line was one of Pop's. In his later years when a driver carried Pop to work and back, he would stop at a bar for a shot of the bar's best whiskey. Apparently both father and son—each of whom had been energetic in his youth—discovered the stimulating effect of a drink on an aging body.

Besides working with Pete, Uncle Lloyd exercised his building and carpentry skills to restore the Iron Rock School, a vintage one-room, brick schoolhouse that was located on the farm. Outfitting it with a sleeping loft, a bathroom, a kitchen, a dining area, a sitting room with a fireplace, and a back porch, he appointed the place with antiques throughout. On two walls, he displayed antique implements, family photos, and memorabilia of the old days. Off the back porch, he erected a swimming pool with a deck. Behind the pool he built a footbridge across a stream, cleared a path several hundred yards through the woods, and set up a park bench with a lock-and-key box in which he stored some bottled spirits and tumblers. Anyone who knew him realized what fun he had designing and creating that shady nook as a sylvan surprise for visitors. Soon, the schoolhouse became a family retreat—much as the cabin had been decades earlier. For several years Uncle Lloyd and Aunt Sally hosted weekend cookouts, birthday dinners, and holiday celebrations.

In restoring the wholeness of the one-room school, Uncle Lloyd did more than make a space useful again. As I see it, he left his mark on a historic, educational landmark, hoping that we would both revere the place and admire his skillful work on it. On our behalf he left a token of his heritage, an emblem of his faith in schooling, and a place for the family to gather.

Uncle Lloyd carried himself confidently, looked like success, and enjoyed good health until his last years. He always dressed stylishly. So proud was he of his name, his initials—in short, of his heritage and who it meant he was—that he loved to wear expensive neckties and monogrammed shirts, along with colorful handkerchiefs folded in his coat pocket. He had his monogram on fine cotton and linen handkerchiefs. As teenagers, Pete and I were often the beneficiaries of his hand-me-downs when he cleaned up his closet. I still have several of his monogrammed handkerchiefs. While the "W" serves just as well as an "M," I hold onto the handkerchiefs as keepsakes.

Uncle Lloyd also had to wear very expensive orthopedic shoes. Moreover, he had to buy them frequently, because he needed the support of a stiff sole. Consequently, whenever he broke them in, he had to stop wearing them and buy new ones. He was forever looking for someone in the family to whom he could give his castaway shoes. I remember trying them on for months, hoping to grow into them. Finally, when my feet were the right size—in my early teens—I got a couple of pairs. I selected one especially good pair for Sunday shoes and took them up to Joe Ferranti for new soles and heels. Joe took one look at the shoes and asked me accusingly, "Where did you ever get shoes like these?" When I explained that they were my Uncle Lloyd's hand-me-downs, he smiled.

Uncle Lloyd's collection of rings, cuff links, tiepins, and lapel pins would have been the envy of any baronet. He also had several belts, suspenders, and garter belts. I rarely saw him wear suspenders, but I frequently spotted his garter belts, which he truly needed. Like the other Wright men, he had a hefty calf muscle on a relatively short leg. His hose—and I do mean elegant men's hosiery—were of a fine woven material that needed support to stay up on that stout leg.

Yes, Uncle Lloyd was his father's first son, his progeny. Not having children of his own to whom he could pass on his birthright, however, he played "father" to hundreds of schoolchildren—and foremost to his nieces and nephews. He was a conservator of his heritage, as an uncle, as a principal of a high school, as a leader of Boy Scouts, as a member of fraternal orders, as a conservative Republican, as a restorer of a turn-of-the-century, one-room schoolhouse, as a composer of our family tree, and as disseminator of the Wright family coat of arms. Ever working to pass on the culture to us, he encouraged my brother and me in our Demolay membership and my sister in Rainbow Girls. However, by the time I came of age, the world had radically changed from the one he knew and loved, and I was destined—by birth, by upbringing, and by personal choice—to become a different sort of man. Nonetheless, I owe to him an understanding of one of manhood's finest exemplars. That I never acknowledged this debt to him during his lifetime burdens me. Moments of silence, filled with unspoken thoughts, are as irrevocable as words thoughtlessly uttered.

Irony has a way of painfully twisting itself into the warp and woof of our lives. Both Uncle Lloyd and Aunt Sally devoted their lives to educating young people, to raising the next generations of Americans. Both of them were so devoted to genealogy, the study of the descent of their families. And, pointedly, the two of them were denied any children of their own. Nobody in the family knew what personal hurt they may have suffered on this account, for they never so much as mentioned the subject. Moreover, part of Uncle Lloyd's motivation to compose the lengthy family tree was his concern that descendants of one of the newer family branches be made aware of their Wright-McKay heritage. In the letter, he wrote, "Recently, Sally and I attended the wedding of our niece, Susan McKay, to one Michael Alan

Ostaphenko." After going on at length about the new couple, their occupations, and their honeymoon plans, Uncle Lloyd remarked, "Why do I get carried away— well because my point is—will their kids always be Ostaphenkos." With that, he discussed the Wright coat of arms and presented the annotated family tree.

By the way, for the record, he also got a crest of the McClelland coat of arms, which features nine lighted lamps, three crescents, and two figures in a boat. Giving the patch to Mary Jane, he joked, "The two monkeys in the boat are Pete and Ben."

As I have been thinking and writing about Uncle Lloyd's life, I now understand that I am more indebted to him than I had thought. The realization came as I spent so much time writing about the old folks, the Wright-Lloyd lineage, and the Wright coat of arms. Not only do I love their life stories simply as fascinating tales that reveal human nature, but, beyond that, I see now that I am a man intrigued by heritage, as Uncle Lloyd was—only for different reasons. For him, the issue of identity resided in the certainty of knowing who he was genealogically with an emphasis on station and pedigree. Heritage was consanguineous in the relational sense. He came from these people and he was of them.

He knew them well and he closely identified with them as people whose stories were as familiar as his own.

For me, the issue of identity springs from my having been fatherless. Knowing my heritage resolves some of my anxiety over an uncertain identity. It is consanguineous, but more abstractly in a psychological, non-relational sense. I am from these people, yet I am not of them. Being of a later generation, I did not know most of them, and I identified with their stories in the sense that they had made their way in a difficult world and had established—more than just peopled—the maternal side of my family. Indeed, my interest in telling any of my relatives' stories that antedate my birth is to discover personal traits and characteristics that, in some way or other, contribute to—rather than constitute—who I am. Knowing my heritage in this sense means defining identity less based on genealogy in the strictly genetic sense. Rather, it is more a matter of interest in the results of a commingling of nature and nurture within the contingencies of certain times and places. Given this definition of heritage, one can understand Aunt Sally's mighty influence on my identity, even though she occupies only an oblique line in my family tree.

In my earliest recollections of Aunt Sally, she is seated at our kitchen table, eating a bite of sandwich, drinking a cup of black coffee, and smoking a cigarette. Daily over her thirty-plus-year career as a teacher at our high school, she walked the two blocks to 201 to take her short lunch break. A creature of habit, she always had a cigarette and a cup of coffee when she was relaxing. Grandma Wright, of course, routinely put a full lunch on the table—sandwiches, hot soup, salad, and, for the hearty appetites, some leftovers from a previous dinner. However, Aunt Sally ate like a bird. Regarding soup, she quoted her favorite aunt, who thought that eating it— spoonful by spoonful—was just too much work. When the awareness of tobacco's dangers became our country's mantra, Aunt Sally simply blew smoke at it. Mom, who was always fond of quoting health tips that she'd read, once reported to Aunt Sally that a study showed you could add seven years to your life if you stopped smoking. Aunt Sally responded, "Seven extra years of life without smoking wouldn't be worth living."

Aunt Sally got the seven extra years and then some— smoking all the while. She survived Uncle Lloyd by ten years, but they were ten very lonely years for her, because she and Uncle Lloyd had been inseparable during their lives. Except for working in different schools, they personified togetherness. They commuted to work together sixty miles daily. Everything they did, they did as partners; everywhere they went, they moved in tandem. Toward the end of her life, when Aunt Sally became seriously ill, my sister—who was also nursing Mom at this time—tended to Aunt Sally's needs. From her hospital bed, Sally confided in Mary Jane that she'd lived too long. Then, in a rare act of generosity, Aunt Sally removed her wedding rings and gave them to Mary Jane, telling her to keep them.

For her part, Mary Jane felt that she couldn't keep the rings. Believing that Aunt Sally may have been too weak to act responsibly, Mary Jane returned the rings to Aunt Sally's jewelry box, appreciating, nevertheless, the unusual act of generosity. Aunt Sally and Uncle Lloyd always favored boys, and Aunt Sally dealt especially severely with girls. This applied within the family as well as without. As youngsters, Pete and I could do no wrong, with a few exceptions, such as the Crocky Morris incident; Mary Jane and Cousin Rosemary, on the other hand, always had to be on their guard. Another thing made the ring-giving unusual: while Aunt Sally left her considerable wealth to her brother, she left no personal items to anybody. She willed that all of her furniture, her household items, and even her most cherished keepsakes be sold at public auction.

What power adults wield over the lives of children in their charge! Aunt Sally was a dominant force in our family, one with which we had to contend even as we grew beyond childhood. Because I moved away from home following high school and because I developed ideological views that opposed those of my conservative family, my relationship with Aunt Sally was strained more than hers with my brother and my sister, who remained in the region and in the fold. Just as she granted me her approbation for my career in education, still she censured me for being a wayward thinker: politically liberal, racially tolerant. Aunt Sally always claimed you as kith, but she also held you accountable to kindred standards.

8

"GET SOME BLACK-SEEDED SIMPSON FOR US TO SOW, BENNY"

Harbison Avenue
Masontown, Pennsylvania

Those who engage in joyous love often must endure its shocking loss. The ones affected most powerfully by both experiences are the innocent, generous souls, those of tender heart and deep passion. In our family my dad's mother was such a figure. A striking young woman from a prominent family, she gradually lost her way in the world, and then eventually lost her health. Through it all she clung to a steadfast faith in God.

We kids never knew why she became progressively unable to read the compass points, why she lost her mental sharpness. My brother seemed to have the best guess: "Grandma Carrie never got over our dad's death." That hunch was all we had to go on until the phone call with Dad's younger brother, Uncle Jim, who had just turned eighty. I hadn't seen or spoken to him in over twenty years. My sister, on the other hand, had visited him and Grandma at his home in Florida just before Grandma died, had exchanged cards with him regularly, and had occasionally spoken with him on the phone.

Mary Jane dialed his number, greeted him, explained that we wanted some information about our dad and about Grandma, and handed the receiver to me. After breaking the ice with pleasantry, we began talking in earnest about family history as if there had never been a decades-long hiatus. He spoke in a friendly but educated, almost formal, manner, carefully enunciating his words and pacing them in a measured way. Several minutes into the hour-long conversation, when I explained that we had been speculating about what caused Grandma Carrie's plight, he revealed a family secret that helped us understand, after all these years, part of what sent Grandma Carrie askew. When he told it, I clapped my hand over my mouth and stared, bug-eyed, at my sister.

"One night when I was a youngster, I was awakened by a commotion downstairs in the kitchen. When I went down, Mother and Father were having a terrible argument. I heard her using language on him that she never spoke. When my father saw me come down the stairs, he ordered me to go back to bed. But Mother said, 'No, come in here, James. I want you to hear all of this.'

"She proceeded, using awful language (Mother was a Sunday school teacher for years and years) to accuse him of cheating on her. She told him how disappointed she was in him. She said she had devoted herself to our family and this was how he treated her. She vowed never to sleep with him again."

Besides revealing the secret, Uncle Jim chatted on, giving us more details about Dad and the family. Uncle Jim recalled, with a note of complaint, that during their high school years the family's routine revolved around my dad's year-round sports schedule: football, basketball, and baseball. Local athletes were valued as blue-ribbon stock and Dad became well known as a talented and tough competitor. In all his high school years as center on the football team, he was out of the lineup only briefly when he suffered a broken arm. Mom was good friends with Dad and his older sister Anna; they were in the same high school class and Sunday school class. Mom and Dad sang together in school programs, with Anna accompanying them on the piano.

Dad, who also liked to hunt, had a bird dog that Uncle Jim claimed Dad neglected until hunting season; all other times Jim was expected to take care of it. Among Dad's firearms was a Mazda rifle with a telescopic sight. He especially loved hunting small game with Doc Wells and his boys.

If Dad wasn't playing hard, he was working hard. In Uncle Jim's words, Dad was always industrious. As a schoolboy, he had a paper route and delivered the Uniontown *Morning Herald*. When he decided to go to college, Dad was expected to pay his own way. He worked in the mine with Grandpa, saving up until he had enough money for a year of school. He attended college in Berkeley, California, studying optometry. A newspaper reported his college as the University of Southern California. According to Uncle Jim, Dad attended a Berkeley branch of the University of California at Los Angeles. To be sure, Dad was on the Berkeley campus: he is pictured in a photograph walking through the famed arch, carrying a leather-bound notebook which my brother now has and in which are listed the telephone numbers of several local coeds. Dad rented a room from a Mrs. Rawlings, according to Uncle Jim, who also recalls that on one occasion when Dad was returning home on a Greyhound bus which stopped for a while in Salt Lake City, he took a walk down the wrong way and was robbed. He had to sell some of his textbooks in order to resume his bus ride home. Nobody remembers how Dad arrived at his choice of optometry as a profession or of the university on the West Coast, but during and after high school he had spent a lot of weekend time with Doc Wells, driving him on house calls—even waiting in the car for hours during a childbirth call once—just to be able to talk things over with Doc during the ride.

At the end of his first year at Berkeley, Dad returned home to work with his father in the Hecla Coal Company's Bessemer mine. He worked at other odd jobs as well. For example, he ran a peanut business out of the family home. He bought large barrels of roasted peanuts, sacked them in one-pound bags and, with

Uncle Jim at the wheel of his Plymouth, sold and delivered them to the local bars. After saving enough money, he went back to school for a couple of more terms.

Returning home after the 1937–38 academic year, Dad began mining again and—with Mrs. Wells making the match—he started dating Mom, who had begun teaching school. Because his little brother Les was in Mom's second-grade classroom, Dad and Mom used Les as a messenger boy. The arrangement worked well for quite some time, until once Les forgot to tell Mom that Dad would be picking her up for a date that evening. When Dad arrived, he caught Mom completely unawares and she had to scramble to get ready. After that, Dad pinned a note to Les's sweater, as did Mom in making a reply.

Dad's connection with the military began when he attended a civilian training camp at Camp Meade, Maryland, at the age of sixteen; he received a certificate and was recommended for advanced training. In 1941, when the war began raging in Europe, he left college for the last time and enlisted in the army, well before the Japanese attack on Pearl Harbor.

Despite their estrangement, Grandma and Grandpa McClelland remained in the same house, raising four children in a loveless home. My dad, the apple of their eye, left for the war front in October of his twenty-ninth year and was killed a few weeks later, compounding the weight bearing down on Grandma Carrie's already-heavy heart. "She never accepted that he died," Uncle Jim said, confirming Pete's conjecture. "She always expected him to come home."

Grandpa had still other women friends, further humiliating Grandma. However, when I was young, I knew none of this and Grandma didn't betray any of her hurt. She and I spent a lot of time working the earth together. Breaking ground for our new garden each spring was our renewal ritual. I remember one Saturday morning in April when I was around eleven.

Unknotting a soiled, lace handkerchief with her rough, work-worn hands, Grandma Carrie selected two dimes to press into my small palm.

"Go to Preach Smith's and get some black-seeded Simpson for us to sow, Benny."

It was early spring and although we would surely have another frost or two, still we could get the lettuce started. Grandma always put in a big garden, as did her neighbors. The Markers and De Bolts put them in their backyards. Uncle Les cultivated a potato patch in a spacious lot behind Fred Walters' backyard. Traveling the back alley was an easy bike ride uptown to Smith's Hardware Store, except for pumping up the last hill. Inside the store, I waited impatiently, standing beside the warm potbellied stove, as Flick slowly poured the tiny seeds into a measuring glass. He treated them as if they were grains of gold. When he handed me the brown paper envelope, I stuffed it in my back pocket, dashed out the back door, and raced back to Grandma's. On my errand I noticed little of the bustling uptown life, as I cherished the thought of turning over the cold, dark, shiny earth, while listening to Grandma reminisce again about her country upbringing.

I had heard her recollections before, of course, but working the ground at the edge of the garden next to where the new rhubarb shoots had already sprouted, I relished hearing them again as she recalled anew her childhood on her father's large farm twenty miles to the northeast. His rhubarb patch ran for yards and yards with rows of plants whose stalks were as long and thick as a child's arm. As a girl, she watched the men from the big hotel in Uniontown cut and trim the stalks, filling baskets and loading them in their wagon. Coming for rhubarb, strawberries, and greens marked their first visit to the farm since late last fall. They returned time and time again throughout the growing season for the produce that Benton Frost's farm yielded. Although Grandma never saw money change hands, she said her father's business with the hotel kept them going. Mom disputed this point some years later, when I told her the story. She contended that old man Frost was probably paying off debts with the vegetables. Saying that she had heard a lot about old man Frost's ways from Dad, Mom called him a wastrel who squandered the huge farm and the family wealth that he had inherited. In our phone conversation, Uncle Jim emphasized his grandfather's work: "He took care of horses for the mine, a very responsible job." My brother recalls talk of another side to the Frost begetter: "He played the fiddle, raised fox-hounds, and rode to the hunt. He died of pneumonia that he caught while foxhunting."

When our lettuce came up in Grandma's backyard plot, she sat on the grass at the garden's edge, pinching off the tender green leaves and putting them in her out-spread apron. Nothing tasted better to her, she said, than some fresh greens. I preferred the early strawberries. Well, truth be told, I always favored the strawberries, early or late. Pete reminded me of our filching some of Grandma's strawberries on a hot, very bright, sunny day. He wrote, "Everyone was inside the house with the doors and windows closed and shaded to keep the heat out. But it wasn't too hot for us to get into mischief. You, Mary Jane, and I had an empty sack, a two-pound Domino sugar bag. The three of us picked strawberries out of Grandma's patch and filled the bag. Mary Jane's little hands barely reached around the sack full of berries. We tried to sell it to one or more of the neighbors. We had a discussion about the price. I think we talked over ten or fifteen cents and agreed on ten cents. Don't know if we went to more than one neighbor or not. Someone, probably Mrs. Marker, told us to take the strawberrries back to Grandma. They were very ripe and pretty well crushed up by then, but she could make jelly with them." In the fall she put up food to live on the whole year, vegetables from her garden and fruit from her trees—peach, cherry, pear, quince, and apple. She scoured the ground, picking up every usable fruit, even if she had to cut out rotten spots. When I asked, once, why she wasted her time peeling even the smallest apples to cook up and can, she replied, "We have to use whatever God provides, Benny."

God also provided those trees for our recreation, so we kids thought. In the summers, our two cousins, the Daileys, joined in the fun. The large apple tree was especially good for climbing. We each liked to perch on different large branches and play games. Breaking up small wooden boxes for seats and using some roofing shingles and roofing nails, we hammered permanent perches in every conceivable place. We had lookouts in all directions and from various heights. After a busy day of war games, it was so satisfying to sit in our seats and munch on the sweet, golden apples. One evening, at Teddy Dailey's urging, we boys had an apple-throwing contest. We each sharpened a stick, put an apple on the point, and flung the apple at the Walters' attic window to see who could hit it. Of course, one of us eventually broke it and all of us got in Dutch for the prank.

We had plenty of fun running around the spacious yard, too. We used one of Grandpa's empty, fifty-gallon, cardboard feed barrels as our own amusement park ride. We rolled it up to the lilac bush border at the top of the side yard. Taking turns, we climbed inside, bracing our arms and legs against the sides. Others gave a big push and we rolled—screaming like banshees all the way—until we finally came to a slamming stop in the privet hedge at the front of the yard.

At night after dinner and baths, we five cousins piled into two beds in the front upstairs bedroom. With the windows open to catch a breeze, we often heard the singing and stomping on the back porch next door. The Markers were hill folks who entertained themselves with a brand of Irish-descended music. We were dog-tired from our long day of playing, and the music neither amused nor bothered us for very long till we drifted off, deaf to the melodies, and the crickets' chirping, and the bullfrogs' croaking.

Grandma Carrie's was a great place to play, but we also had fun putting ourselves to work. Throughout our youth, we kids each maintained our own summer garden plot there. My brother and I earned Boy Scout merit badges and other awards for our gardening. Pete was better at it than I—more scientific and more thoroughgoing—but in his late teens, Pete had lots of other things occupying his time: football, cars, buddies, and girlfriends. I continued to visit Grandma and to work in the garden. Whether she admired my gardening or just appreciated my company, Grandma told others that I was good at it, saying emphatically, "When Benny plants an onion, it grows."

A dozen or so years later, when my fraternity brothers headed to Florida for spring break, I returned home from college and headed out to Grandma Carrie's to turn over the soil for her. Though we were both greatly changed, we still had that same bond to the soil—and to each other. Again, some years after that, when I held my first teaching job, I returned to help get the garden started, planting black-seeded Simpson lettuce, early peas, and the initial group of onion bulbs.

Today, I enjoy landscape gardening. Whether I just walk around, pinching off deadheads and pulling a few weeds, or whether I design and put in a whole new accent plot, I feel restored by the labor. Even though I spade up red clay soil these days, I still think of Grandma Carrie and me in another world and time— in love with each other and the good earth.

I never consciously began looking for my dad's traits in his father until sometime after Grandpa's sudden death from a heart attack one evening following work in 1957, when he was just days shy of his sixty-second birthday. Of course, knowing my grandpa only in the last decade of his life, I did not see him at his best.

Born in 1895, when events leading to the Spanish-American War began heating up, Ewing Clyde McClelland grew up on a farm in Keister, Pennsylvania. Just three years later, when stories of the war were still in the local newspaper, so was a story about Grandpa's family succumbing to fever. Living on the Huston farm in North Union Township, the family had contracted the illness from bad well water. Grandpa's dad and many of his seven siblings died, though Grandpa, his mother, and two of his sisters survived. With a setback like that at such an early age, Grandpa must have had to make his own way in life, but we never heard any particulars. Although we kids never knew of her at the time, one of Grandpa's sisters apparently lived in south Masontown throughout our childhood.

In stature, Grandpa and my dad were similarly tall and well-muscled, strong though slender. Both had fine facial features, including fair complexions, handsome noses, and prominent chins. Grandpa had ice-blue eyes, a trait that none of his dark-eyed children inherited. He wore rimless spectacles to read. And his once-dark hair had thinned considerably, turning pure white.

As a young man, Grandpa distinguished himself by winning a foot race on the gravel road from Uniontown to Brownsville. By the time I saw his large victor's cup, it was deeply tarnished, but its presence in the house was a reminder that my dad's athletic prowess was inherited.

Grandpa courted Carrie, one of the attractive, dark-eyed Frost twins who belonged to a prominent farming family near Searights Crossing. Sitting atop a ridge, the Frost mansion was visible from the highway. It was a popular spot for the social set. As Uncle Jim explained, they folded back the wooden walls separating the bedrooms, pushed the furniture back, rolled up the carpets, brought in musicians or cranked up the Victrola, and held grand dances in the large, makeshift ballroom. Long after the place had passed into other hands, friends of the Frosts still talked about the house with its massive chandelier in the entryway and an elaborate stairway to the second floor.

When Grandpa's attentions to Grandma Carrie began looking serious, Grandma once told Mary Jane, her family sent her off to stay at a distant relative's farm across the county to hide her away. They had in mind a man of higher social standing. However, Grandpa stayed the course, learned when she returned home, and persisted in making suit, getting her to agree to a tryst. Grandma told me of this adventure a half-century later when, after church one Sunday, I drove her out of Fayette County across the bridge over the Monongahela River into Greene County, to see Pete's new farm. She protested, insisting that I take her home, but I told her to relax and enjoy the ride. After she realized that I was not about to turn around, she sat back and said, "The first time I crossed this river was on the ferry with Poppy in his buggy." She went on to explain that he took her on a daylong outing to the Greene County Fair. In 1913, they married. He was eighteen and she a year younger. Promptly, they began filling the house with children, two in about as many years and a third about six years later.

To be closer to his good-paying mine job, Grandpa moved his bride into a rented house on North Main Street in Masontown. While he worked a shift in the mine each day, in the evenings and on weekends he labored to finish out the house that he was building for her on Harbison Avenue, the last residential street off North Main Street. Given who she was, though, Grandma couldn't bear living in that little rented house.

She wanted to live in her own two-story house. And she wanted to do so at that very moment. Grandpa reassured her that the house would be ready in a few months. However, having already used up what little patience she had, and having a mind of her own about such things, Grandma moved their furnishings and belongings into the unfinished house one day while Grandpa was working his shift. The rooms on the first floor were walled in, but it had only a subflooring; the second-floor rooms weren't yet finished out. Nevertheless, Grandma could say that she was living in her new house in town, even if it took some time before Grandpa could complete the building. He never did finish the flooring, which accounted for its always being so cold in winter.

For his part, in those early years, Grandpa kept Grandma outfitted in the style to which she had been accustomed. "Mother had two fur coats, several pretty hats, and fine velvet dresses," Uncle Jim assured me. During the family's early years, Aunt Anna, Dad, and Uncle Jim were raised by a beautiful, happy mother. So protective was Grandma of Aunt Anna that she held her out of school for a year, until Dad became old enough for first grade. That way, Dad and Aunt Anna walked together the three miles to school and back. The children played board games with their mother, listened to records on the Edison player, danced, and sang. When the other-woman incident changed things, the child affected most was Les, who was born much later and who reported feeling unloved by his mother. Ironically, Grandma called Les "Honey Boy" throughout his days with her.

I wish I had more and better memories of Grandpa McClelland. One encounter particularly stained my memory of him. Grudgingly, he let me raise a pup out at his place. Predictably, I called this white, short-hair, mixed-breed "Whitey." I kept her chained to a doghouse next to the pigeon coop. But I let her run free a lot when I went out to the house. A problem arose when she coupled with a neighbor's dog. Long afterwards, I retold the incident in a short story. Although I sentimentalized the story as a dialogue between my cousin Nancy and me on the day of Grandpa's funeral, the essential details are accurate.

> When Benny sat next to her, Nancy turned on him. "Why are you crying? You didn't even like Poppy?"

"I'm crying because he made me hurt Whitey's pups and she left me. I forgot about all that until your dad started putting the dirt on top of his coffin."

"What are you talking about?"

"You don't know. You only come here for Christmas and summer vacation. But don't you remember my Whitey that I kept at Grandma's a couple of years ago?"

"Yeah. So what?"

"Well, she used to get together with some of the neighbors' dogs. You know what I mean. Once two of them were stuck together. Grandpa took a bucket of creek water and threw it on them to separate them. He called her a 'no 'count mongrel bitch' that day. She had five pups on Easter. I found them when we went to Grandma's after the sunrise service. Whitey had them under the pigeon coop. Grandpa got a spade and a feed sack. He told me I had to drown them in the creek or he was going to throw them off the bridge into the river the way he did with the litters of cats.

"I took Whitey to Grandma and asked her to keep Whitey with her at the house. I played with the pups until they tired and fell asleep. Then I put them in the sack and held them under the creek water until my wrists ached and my hands went numb."

"You drownded them?"

"'Drowned' them. I drowned them so I could bury them. Grandma said I gave them a good Christian burial. 'Cause he was just going to throw them in the river. I had to put flagstone over their grave to keep Whitey from digging them up. She ran away later that spring and I think it's because I hurt her pups. He made me. That hurt came back when your dad put the dirt on him today. I got clay balls in my shoes today, too, just like that day when I buried the pups. You cry for him. You were his pet. I was crying for Whitey's hurt. And my dad's. And mine."

"Well, stop being so selfish. Today's Poppy's day."

"Nancy, leave him alone," my sister insisted. "He takes burying hard."

I included the last few lines here—though I now wince at the maudlin display—because they reveal that even at thirty-something, when I wrote this piece, I connected memories of all personal losses with the loss of my dad. This childhood memory was one of my few distinctly unhappy ones. And, although I had no rational reason for thinking Dad would have reacted any differently to the situation from how Grandpa had, I thought my dad would have been so much kinder to me, because he would have been a much younger man and he would have been my father, not my grandfather.

Among us kids, my brother, Pete, has the best memories of Grandpa. Two years older, he frequented the

McClelland house sooner and more regularly than Mary Jane and I did while Grandpa was still alive. After we twins were born and Dad returned to his military base, Grandma Carrie insisted on helping out by coming up to 201 every morning to bathe us. However, one day when she was away from her place, the pigs got out of the pen and caused a good deal of damage in the neighbors' yards. (Dad had brought the first piglet to their place when he was a boy. After he had helped Elliott Christopher with some chores around his place, Elliott paid him with a piglet.) After the pigs tore up the neighborhood, Grandpa said that Grandma had better stay at home. Intent on helping out with her absent son's children, Grandma sent Les to our house daily to bring Petie back in a stroller. So, as a toddler, Petie spent most of his days with the McClellands. When he got big enough to walk the mile by himself, he danced a jig until Mom dressed him and sent him on his way, skipping out to the north end of town. As he grew older, Pete followed Grandpa around, watching him work under the hood of his Buick or on the tiller's Briggs and Stratton engine.

Grandpa was fond of raising chickens, ducks, geese, and pigeons. Always glad to start others out, he lent our first cousin Bruce Sterling an incubator and showed him how to brood and raise his first poults. When my brother was about nine or ten, he took an interest in acrobatic pigeons and Grandpa encouraged him, letting him use an old brooder house and showing him all of the ins and outs of raising them, including how to prepare a squab for dinner.

In our fifties, when Pete and I talked about Grandpa, he recalled a couple of stories that I had never heard. As a pit boss, Grandpa took a crew into the mine, marked a chalk line on the wall at the face, and oversaw the digging and hauling of coal. In the darkness of the mine, the men had to make their way the best they could by the weak yellow light of the carbide lamps on their helmets. During lunch break the men would stay in the pit, lean against the wall to ease their aching backs, and eat from their metal lunchboxes. A man who liked his coffee, Grandpa carried sandwiches in the top portion of the box, but had the larger, lower section filled with coffee. At the end of the day when they loaded their tools back in the wagon, Grandpa measured the distance from the chalk line to the new face wall, because the company paid the crew by the number of feet it mined. To take the measurement, Grandpa stood at the first line holding a tape measure and had one of his men pull the end of the tape to the new face wall. At the end of one shift, the number on the tape seemed high to Grandpa, but he couldn't see through the dusty darkness to the face wall. When he rolled in the tape, he noticed that the last couple of feet were crumpled up. Suspicious, he asked the man to measure the distance again. This time, he watched the man closely and caught him wadding up the tape in his hand as he walked.

"Why, you're nothing more than a gangster!" Grandpa exclaimed. The man was fired, of course, but soon found work elsewhere. However, the news of his run-in with Grandpa traveled with him. For the rest of his days he was always called "Gangster."

No doubt Grandpa or Les told Pete that story, but the next one Pete got firsthand from Old Rooster. When we kids were about ten or so, the state built a new highway that cut through Grandpa's northernmost acreage, leaving just the outbuildings and garden plots directly behind the house. The new roadway was elevated about thirty feet above the surrounding land, and the state sowed the steep embankment in grass that required cutting—in this case with a scythe. One day when Pete was playing out back, he noticed a black man cutting the grass above the property. The man stopped to rest and spotted Pete, asking whose boy he was. When he replied that Pete McClelland was his grandpa, the man drew back and looked toward the house. Then, the man told Pete that one time Grandpa had called him something at work, so he hauled off and hit Grandpa in the mouth, knocking out his tooth. "He got me fired, but I hit him a good one. You tell him that you saw Old Rooster." Pete never mentioned the incident to Grandpa, fearing his reaction. He figured that Grandpa had said something about Old Rooster being a lazy so-and-so, resulting in the punch, and Pete didn't want to stir up any bad memories.

Both Pete and I remember watching Grandpa turn over the earth with the large, yellow tiller he used for gardening. Grandpa occasionally took a break from the work, walked to the shady side of the chicken coop, and stood with his back and one foot propped against it to smoke a cigarette. Grandma had outlawed smoking in the house, so sometimes in the evening he'd also walk up the narrow brick pathway from the house, squat against the coop, and look over the garden as he smoked.

That pose of Grandpa, smoking alone with his back against the chicken coop, seems to me like a metaphor for his life—at least what I knew of it. Unlike the gregarious Wrights, he was a solitary, taciturn man, who kept his thoughts to himself. I do not ever recall Grandpa attending church, although Grandma did faithfully. On the other hand, he seemed to enjoy the company of his growing family—at least for a while. I recall eating large family dinners at the house when his children brought the other grandchildren to visit. He had limited patience for us noisy kids. After one too many of our shenanigans, he would bark at us to stop the ruckus and go outside to play.

Grandpa continued philandering throughout his life, even up to the moment when he dropped dead from an aneurysm after returning home from work one night. The next morning, as Grandma went to tend to the coal furnace, she found him at the foot of the basement steps still in his work clothes. Uncle Jim said that he and Aunt Anna's husband followed Grandpa one night, trying to locate this last woman's whereabouts, but that Grandpa lost them on the road. I only learned of the mistress's existence because I heard it told later that she showed up at Grandpa's funeral, asking if he mentioned her in his will. She apparently had expected him to do so and was disappointed to learn that he had not. Mom said that they found receipts and check stubs confirming that Grandpa had regularly bought groceries for this woman and took care of her rent. Whatever Grandma may have known about the last mistress, she never let on.

In her later years Grandma Carrie turned daffy, simpleminded. Who knows whether Grandma's gradual childlike turn resulted partly from Grandpa's womanizing? Who knows the grief she carried after losing her son, her pride and joy? Late in her life she continued to bake, even though nobody was there to enjoy it and even though she no longer made the cookies and rolls very well. Did she just scrimp on the ingredients or did she forget how to bake them? Out of habit she continued quilting, darning socks, knitting, and sewing—and, of course, gardening. She talked to herself, whistled, or sang all the while. She boiled up a small mess of green beans that served as her dinner. She ate from a pot of cold vegetables that sat on the kitchen table until she eventually finished them off. If she ever became ill, she doctored herself. Her trusted remedy was Vicks salve, which she spread liberally on her chest, stuffed up her nose, and even swallowed by the spoonful.

In her dotage, the muscles in her right eye let it turn outward. Her thinning gray hair hung in wisps around her ears. Wrapped up in several layers of aging dresses and worn sweaters, she clattered around in the house in men's shoes with overrun heels. In winter, she let her house stay ice cold, so she wouldn't have to buy another load of coal for the furnace. Whenever one of us stopped in to visit, we went to the basement first and shoveled in several scoops of coal to fire up the furnace. She didn't like to venture out of the house to go any-where, except to church faithfully every Sunday. She customarily showed up at our house more than an hour before Sunday school began; she refused to come upstairs, but sat inside the door on the stairs—thumb-ing through her Bible—until time for the church doors to open. Occasionally, Mary Jane lured her upstairs and she scratched Mary Jane's back just by rubbing her cal-lused hands over it. Otherwise, Mom went down the stairs, sat beside Grandma, combed her hair, and put some blush on her cheeks. While Mom looked after Grandma Carrie, relations between them had never been keen. Two stubborn women, they apparently had a bit of a tug-o'-war over Dad. In one of his numerous letters to Mom from an army base, Dad explained that

he would not, after all, be able to give her the large, formal portrait he had had made in his dress uniform. He
would have to give it to his mother.

Grandma wouldn't spend her pension money,
depositing all of her checks in her savings account,
except barely enough to pay her utility bills and purchase basic necessities. Over her objections, we kids
drove her uptown to pay her bills. She acted afraid to go
to the window to pay the electric bill. She refused to buy
food herself. When her cupboard was absolutely bare,
she gave Mom fifty cents and asked her to buy some sta-
ples for her. Each time we returned from the grocery
store with several bags full of food, enough to last her a
couple of weeks. Although we worried about her,
Grandma Carrie was so independent that she was hard
to deal with. And she wasn't the Grandma Carrie that
we had known as youngsters. As teenagers lacking
empathy with our elders, we often called her just "Carrie" among ourselves, as if she were one of the many
town characters in our family stories.

Typically, Uncle Jim visited Grandma for a week in
the summer every year. During one visit, he asked her

the whereabouts of several war bonds that he knew she had. She adamantly denied having them. Letting the point drop, he went out to mow the grass. When he returned, Grandma told him—without his asking—that the bonds were under the dresser in the bathroom. He moved the dresser aside, pulled up the linoleum, and found several thousand dollars' worth of bonds. He deposited them for her in the bank and took over her financial affairs.

In my late twenties, when I moved out of the region to pursue my career, I lost touch with Grandma Carrie, except for brief, annual visits. To me she seems a tragic figure. I will always hold the memory of her sitting in her wobbly, low-backed rocker at the south-facing, living room window. Sitting there for light in the otherwise darkened house, she read and reread her Bible, her family Bible, which carried the names and birth dates of all her children. She had lost her eldest son to war. Her husband, who had left off being faithful many years earlier, had died twenty years before. Her daughter, too, had died in her early fifties of a sudden heart attack one fall day when raking leaves. Her youngest son, carrying out a busy schedule as a career air force pilot, was always away. Her remaining son visited once a year. For years, as she remained in an empty house during unending weekdays, she went through the motions of household chores and then sat by that window bent over the Bible.

Years later, after Grandma suffered a stroke, Uncle Jim took her to his Florida home, where he cared for her in her final days. Before they left the house on Harbison Avenue, Uncle Jim gave Mom Dad's formal portrait. Grandma, who had rarely left her home county for seventy years, spent the last few in a tropical land of swamps and tourists. But no matter. Uncle Jim cared well for her. Besides, she had lost her world long before she lost her life.

When I want to cheer myself thinking about Grandma Carrie, I recall the many times my sister and I visited her as youngsters on Saturdays in winter. Entering through the back door, we smelled the spicy, yeasty aroma of cinnamon rolls, dinner rolls, and loaves of bread. One batch of hot cinnamon rolls was already sitting on the table stacked on a Jewel Tea plate, the fall leaf pattern. Another batch was baking. On every available space Grandma had set out more to rise in pans covered with cloths to protect the dough from drafts. In a large pot she was cooking the wide, thick, egg noodles that she had just mixed, rolled out, and cut. In no time we could sample them, steaming hot, in a heavily peppered, chicken-stock gravy.

We played and sang along with the quarter-inch-thick records on her windup Edison player or with the roller tunes on her upright player piano. We also made music ourselves—all three of us seated on the piano bench. With Mary Jane playing accompaniment on the slightly out-of-tune piano, we sang from the church hymnal. Among Grandma's favorites were "The Old Rugged Cross," "Rock of Ages," "The Little Brown Church in the Wildwood," and "The Garden." They became our favorites, too. To this day, whenever I hear those old hymns, I think fondly of Grandma Carrie, who sought succor in God's love.

Rock of Ages, cleft for me, / Let me hide myself in Thee; / Let the water and the blood, / From Thy wounded side which flowed, / Be of sin the double cure; / Save from wrath and make me pure.

9

A CABIN OF FAMILY STORIES

Lake o' the Woods, West Virginia
1946–1954

We stopped going to the cabin at the lake nearly fifty years ago. And it's been about forty years since I last saw it. Well, glimpsed it. It looked small—puny, really—viewed from the four-seater when my brother made a flyover on our way to visit Cousin Tommy Dick. Years later, on a lark, somebody drove up the mountain again, but couldn't locate it. Yet the cabin still lives within us all, the locus of a significant period in our family's history. We keep it alive—as we have all our valuable moments—through storytelling.

I don't remember anything of the cabin's beginning. I learned of it piecemeal years later as the men told stories after Sunday dinners at home, long after the cabin had been sold. But despite truth's matter-of-factness, I needed to envision its beginning from a slightly different perspective.

They built it in a single summer during the days following World War II, bittersweet days for Mom: her brothers and her brother-in-law returned home from the war against Hitler, but her husband did not. Mom's second-oldest brother, my uncle Tom, who had taken over the family automobile dealership business from Pop, bought the lakefront property in northern West Virginia for a mountain retreat. An avid fisherman, Pop was aging. This would be someplace closer to home where he could enjoy his sport.

Uncle Tom procured wood from army surplus matériel. As barracks were dismantled, the beams and boards, windows and doors were sold for use in building homes, businesses, and in this case, a summer cabin. When a teamsters' strike shut out all truck traffic into Pittsburgh, Uncle Tom learned that a truck driver who was parked at a roadside rest on the Pennsylvania Turnpike was looking for someone to buy his load of building material. He was eager to unload and get his truck on the road again. Uncle Tom struck a deal with the driver and led him to the cabin site, where, with the help of several mechanics from the shop, they unloaded and stacked the wood.

They set up several army tents on the hillside. Some protected the wood from the elements. Others housed the men as they worked throughout that summer. When the cicadas arrived—we called them seven-year locusts—they inhabited the tents as well as the trees. Uncle Tom and Aunt Rose's kids, my cousins Tommy Dick and Rosemary, thought the locusts were great fishing bait. I remembered the next infestation when we collected the empty shells that we found attached to tree bark.

Although it belonged to Uncle Tom and Aunt Rose, from beginning to end the cabin was a family affair. Pop and his three sons were all expert carpenters. With Pop planning and supervising each day's work, the brothers threw themselves into digging and pouring footers, erecting the frame, and nailing on the sides and roof. They hired a plumber, a cabinetmaker, and a stonemason. Others pitched in from time to time, but the cabin rose out of the skill, strength, and dogged persistence of an aging father and his three sons.

For Pop, a self-taught engineer, it was the familiar challenge of creating something useful and beautiful. In his prime he had supervised the building of imposing, multipurpose structures for his business and for our home as well as for his community government, which he headed for over two decades. This job was different, however. It was an opportunity to work with his sons as grown men, reunited after a long separation during the war years—years of uncertainty and worry, through which Pop sat night after night in his radio room, listening to the day's news reports, hoping to learn how his two younger sons were faring in the battles across the sea. Now, he could displace anxiety with good, hard work, as he measured boards precisely, mitered their ends true, and shouted from the ladder's base to his sons to nail them just so in order to make a solid joint.

For the sons it was the chance to pound away frightful memories, knowing that the claps of sound were their hammers echoing off the woods across the lake, not a round of enemy artillery fire from a nearby ridge. To be sure, there were disputes. Pop was used to calling the shots, no matter what the issue. Uncle Lloyd, the oldest, deferred only to his father. Uncle Tom, three years younger, always suffered the fate of the second born. Even though Tom was younger, it was—as he would remind the others—his damn place! Uncle Ben, fourteen years younger than Uncle Lloyd, was forever demonstrating his individuality. Moreover, having come of age in four years of frontline combat in the 101st Army Airborne Division, he was more independent-minded than ever. Nonetheless, even though these four men's divergent views survived the war intact, they stuck with the project to its completion. There were peacemakers along, too. Tommy Dick pitched in with his ever-cheerful demeanor. My sister, trained by Grandma to please the men in the family, served as the cook, standing on a chair to reach the stove to cook them breakfast.

As I suggested, my remembrance of the cabin's construction varied willfully from others' stories about the building process. No doubt my need to view it this way came from a need to see our family knit together again by family loyalty, following its disruption during the war. If I couldn't have a dad, at least I could have Pop and my uncles resuming a normal family life, recovering from living in a world at war.

What we always called the cabin, others referred to as a lodge: a two-story, white-frame, rectangular structure, with the long side facing the lake. The interior featured knotty-pine walls, built-in corner cupboards, hardwood floors, a small, well-equipped kitchen and a dining area with a long, picnic-style table (also from army surplus). Light splayed from a large wagon-wheel light fixture with frosted-glass chimneys. Adjacent to the dining area, the spacious living room held a large sofa and overstuffed chairs. At the far wall a magnificent stone fireplace rose twenty feet from floor to ceiling. Three bedrooms were tucked away in the second-story loft, where we kids slept in bunk beds. A master bedroom and bath led off the living room. Antique rugs, stylish lamps, and comfortable furnishings appointed the rooms throughout.

Fed by springs, the green, crystal-clear lake lay 150 yards from the cabin down a gently sloping lawn. When inside, we viewed it from the large living room picture window or through the French doors which led from the dining area. In front of the cabin we could look at the water from a row of assorted lawn chairs. Midway between the cabin and the lake, a heavy brass bell hung on a post, encircled by a love seat. Building this had been Pop's pet project. He obtained a bell from an old locomotive and cut the post from a telephone pole. He painted the post and the wraparound seat white with green trim. The bell was supposed to be reserved for announcing mealtime or calling for help, but we kids loved to run around the seat, ringing it until an adult made us stop.

One of those first summers the lake community's developers cut the levee and drained the lake to allow the residents to build docks. Uncle Les dug the postholes and sank the pilings. My other uncles constructed the frame and laid the plank flooring. The dock measured six feet wide and protruded twenty-five feet into the water. A heavy, tall-backed bench sat at the dock's end—a great fishing spot, if someone else was using the rowboat. One early summer day, when the dock needed repainting, Mom put us kids to work, stripped down to our shorts so we wouldn't ruin our clothes with the oil-based paint. The morning of painting went rapidly; by noon we had coated the dock as well as our hands, arms, legs, and feet. The bright sun had done its job that morning, as well. So, where our skin wasn't painted white, it glowed bright pink. Aunt Rose, Dr. Brady's daughter and one well versed in things curative, always took charge of our medical needs. She scrubbed us with a turpentine-soaked cloth to remove the paint. Oh, did it sting! When they told the story some time later, they said we screamed and jumped as if we had St. Vitus's dance.

After Mom watched in horror as Uncle Tom gave us kids sink-or-swim lessons off the dock, she enrolled us in swimming lessons at the Uniontown YMCA. I remember the dank-smelling, boys' locker room where we self-consciously stripped off our clothes. Because boys wore no swimsuits, we were eager to get in the water for modesty, if not for the lessons. Back at the lake, we swam around the dock, playing tag underneath it, holding onto the slippery pilings and climbing over the wooden braces, where spiders had woven their intricate webs. We never wanted to get out of the water, no matter how cold it was. Mom held out towels and demanded, "Come here this minute! Your lips are blue!" Uncle Tom taught us to dive off the dock, encouraging us with directions: "Point your arms over your head, palms together. Lean over and point your hands at the water. Now, bend your knees and jump!" Holding us by our ankles, he gave us a flip when we jumped to get our legs up and prevent a belly flop. Somehow we finally learned how to dive, although there's no telling how many times Uncle Tom had to flip our legs up until we got the knack.

Nobody enjoyed being in the water more than Mom did. She swam only a little and sunbathed just enough to warm herself. Floating was her specialty. She'd strap on her white rubber bathing cap, walk slowly into the shallow water, gently bathing her arms and legs to get acclimated to the cold water, swim out a ways, roll over on her back, and lie straight out on the surface. With her feet pointed skyward and her head back in the water, only her face and toes were visible from a distance. Whatever body control skill or inner calm it took, Mom had a special gift for it. She could lie there, eyes closed, perfectly composed just bobbing slowly up and down with the waves for hours, so it seemed. She could have written *Zen and the Art of Backfloating*. Sometimes when we kids spotted her as a good target, we swam out and threatened to splash or dunk her. She implored us, "Please let me have some peace." To this day, whenever I float or swim the backstroke, I think of Mom, face to the heavens, restoring herself on the lake's surface.

About twenty yards off the dock's end they had anchored a ten-foot-square float made of planks bolted to a base of fifty-five-gallon drums. My brother and I raced from the dock to the float and back countless times. Finally, he challenged me to race the width of the lake and back. He had already made it over and back once, with Mom and Mary Jane rowing alongside him, begging him, "Stop and get into the boat before you get a cramp and drown." Although I had never tested my endurance for such a distance, I couldn't back down. We waited until no adults were in sight and took off. Of course, he beat me both ways. I really struggled on the return leg, having to roll over on my back several times—gasping for air, kicking, and resting my rubbery arms. It was a foolhardy venture, I know now, but sometimes, when you're the second son, it seems that you have to accept the dare. I swam to save face.

When my brother heard me tell about these competitive adventures later in life, he confessed to feeling guilty for being the older brother, being bigger, and getting to go places without us younger kids. I told him not to fret; I would have done the same if I were the older. Besides, the second mouse gets the cheese. Over the years I learned how to make being younger work for me.

Pete and I competed at rowing the boat, too. It was a safe, flat-bottomed skiff that the Berkshire brothers had built. Years and years later, Pete wrote me about accompanying Pop and Uncle Tom on the visit to Berkshire's carpentry shop down by the Monongahela River:

> I recall being with Pop and Uncle Tom in the workshop at Berkshire's lumber yard. It had to be mid-winter. It was cold and snowing outside and, even though it was after dark, the men were still working in the warm, well-lighted shop. Pop was wearing his heavy tweed overcoat. Uncle Tom was wearing his cashmere overcoat and smoking Pall Malls, even though they asked him to not smoke because the floor was deep with wood shavings and sawdust. I had on hat, coat, and leggings. Harry Berkshire was showing them a rowboat he was building for someone. He pointed out the flat bottom, "Almost impossible to overturn." His sales pitch was good because Uncle Tom said, "I want that boat." Harry told him it was sold and an argument began over the boat. Uncle Tom insisted on buying THAT boat. Finally, Pop said, "Simmer down, Tom." Then Harry agreed to build a boat and I believe the price was $200. It was a very serviceable boat.

Pete and I were always seeing who could row that boat farther. And we always wanted to row for the adults who went out fishing. Doc Wells, who was our aunt Frankie's father, always made fishing fun for us kids. Doc Wells was a country-bred gentleman, beloved physician, spinner of tall tales, tennis player, bird hunter, fisherman, and card player par excellence. Although we didn't know it at the time, he had been very close to our dad when Dad was in high school with Mack, the oldest Wells boy. Doc really liked us kids. He entertained us with jokes and country-wise sayings for things. He always brought a large coffee can of very long night crawlers, which he jokingly called snakes, knowing he would get a giggle out of us. Later, we started calling worms snakes, too, and we laughed and thought of Doc Wells.

I always had a special feeling for Doc Wells because, even though he wasn't our family doctor, he had treated me once in an emergency. One evening at 201, I reached up on the kitchen counter for a cloth towel. I didn't see the cup of tea that Grandma Wright had set on it to steep. The cup hit me below the chest, scalding my midsection. I remember lying in bed with my shirt off, sobbing in pain, and feeling panicky about the two quarter-sized blisters on my reddened stomach. A shadow fell across me and I looked up to see Doc Wells's large frame filling the doorway. He walked over slowly, pulled a chair up, set his little black case on the bedstand, and took my hand.

"How're you feeling, Benny," he said softly, with tobacco-smelling breath.

"I feel real sick to my stomach," I managed to say between weak sobs.

He looked so kindly at me, patted my hand, and said, "Well, seeing you like this makes us all feel kinda sick. Let me try to make you feel better."

His calm manner put me at ease and I relaxed. I enjoyed watching his mustache wiggle when he talked or whistled, which he did softly as he attended to my burn. With a wooden tongue depressor, he gently spread a yellow ointment over my midsection and taped two large gauze bandages over it. He had me take a pill with a drink of water and said, "Now, Benny, you get some rest and you'll be back to running up and down the hall again in no time."

As he left, I heard him instructing Grandma about changing the dressing.

Although I don't remember fishing as much as other things, we apparently did quite a lot, according to family accounts. Pete built a fine collection of poles and tackle over the years. Somehow I learned to bait a hook and to take a fish off the hook without getting stuck by its fins, performing these feats for my squeamish sister, as well. (When we were younger, however, I had relied a lot on that sister for more mundane tasks of manual dexterity: for months she tied shoes for both of us till I finally learned to tie my own.) But fishing isn't as uppermost in my memory as picking berries with Grandma and Aunt Rose, seeing red-haired, fair-skinned Rosemary walking around with dried, cracking buttermilk covering her frequent sunburns, hearing Rosemary shriek after being frightened by a blacksnake, collecting locust shells with Mary Jane, and playing with Bobby, the shy boy next door, whose family Mom said was filthy rich. Bobby's corpulent mother liked how we boys got along together so well that she asked Mom if I could go home with them for a week. Mom said no politely. Later, she admitted that she was afraid of what my being with rich people so long might do to me. Would I become envious? Would I think less of what we had? This could be the worry of any middle-class mother, but no doubt Mom had something specific in mind because of her firsthand experience with the family's loss of wealth. When the family fortune vanished during the Great Depression, she was a teenager and nothing made so drastic a change in her life—until Dad was killed.

While the Tom Wrights owned the cabin and while Aunt Rose and Rosemary stayed there throughout each season, they opened the cabin to the whole family. Indeed, family members held many social events there: Grandma hosted elaborate picnics for the women in her Sunday school class; Mom gave swimming parties for our classmates and the church youth; when the Daileys, our cousins on my dad's side of the family, visited from New York, Mom invited them up for a swim; and business associates and family friends were graciously entertained. Still, for the most part, our stays at the cabin were filled with day after day of solitary time in an out-of-the-way mountain retreat.

For the lake's caretaker, Zeke, and his family, this was home, but for me the lake scene constituted a world distinctly apart from what I knew as home. Driving about an hour to the remote region in northwest West Virginia—miles from the nearest town—we traveled the last few miles on a gravel road. Our world at the lake ran according to natural rhythms. The sun marked time. In the morning, the sun's rise reflected off the green water. Throughout the long day, it moved across the broad sky and it set behind the western ridge. Daily temperatures and changeable weather patterns dictated our activities. And our movements were checked by chance meetings with ancient box turtles, cicadas, snakes, and skunks.

When we heard the infrequent sound of car tires on the gravel, we stopped in our tracks to see who was entering our world. We greeted the carload of friends or relatives as if they were long-lost souls or sojourning pilgrims who had finally arrived at the holy shrine. So it was from staying at the cabin that I first developed a conscious sense of place. Home had been a commonplace scene, simply the locality I had unconsciously inhabited from my birth. Dwelling in the cabin at the lake, however, I had moved into a distinct and notable realm. It was more than just a cabin to my family, too, especially when the world threatened to harm us.

Around 1950 the cabin at the lake became a refuge, a sanctuary from fear. Already on edge from the Red Scare and the seemingly imminent dropping of the atomic bomb, we succumbed to the fear of epidemic. When I was about seven, we were quarantined at the lake for the entire summer, because a poliomyelitis epidemic swept across the country. Our cousin Walter, who lived Up East, and one of my brother's classmates, who lived two blocks away, had contracted the disease. Uncle Tom suggested that Mom take us kids to the mountains in hopes of escaping this dreaded child-crippler. Aunt Rose and Rosemary had also taken Rosemary's friend Patty along.

After a considerable time at our secluded retreat, Mom took us for a drive, seven miles down the mountain road to the nearest civilization, a village called White House. Straddling the state line, White House had a general store with a gas pump out front, some small churches, and assorted houses. After getting gas, sodas, and ice cream cones, we crossed into Pennsylvania, going farther into civilization to the next town, which had a movie house, where we munched on popcorn as we watched a musical. (Mom loved musicals; decades later, when videotapes became available, she bought every musical she could and played them endlessly, losing herself in their idealistic love songs and glamorous romances.)

At the end of the week, when Uncle Tom came to spend the weekend, someone spilled the beans that we had been to a matinee. The famous Wright tempers flared, with him accusing Mom of undermining the whole quarantine scheme, simply because she got bored.

"The children got cabin fever," Mom insisted.

"The children? You mean Marianna! Marianna got cabin fever. That's who got cabin fever!"

They apparently had quite an argument, although we were kept out of earshot. Hearing the story told years later, we found the argument embellished this way or that, depending on the storyteller, comically exaggerating the brother-sister spat. Of course, the adults could afford this playfulness with the tale, because we kids had become protected by the recently discovered polio vaccine. However, during the years of uncertainty, the family's anxiety rarely abated. Throughout it all, we children remained miraculously untouched, although the disease seemed to swirl invisibly all around us and to strike, quite visibly, those close to us. Ironically, after spending the week in the mountains with Rosemary, Patty returned home only to come down with polio. While her illness left no serious consequences, at the time Rosemary and her family worried so, expecting her to come down with the disease, too. She was spared her playmate's fate. Pete's classmate survived his illness, but suffered crippling of one leg, requiring that he wear a brace. Our cousin Walter bravely fought a long, losing battle, including lying for months in an iron lung until he succumbed. So, the fear—more like a cold, foreboding dread for the adults—seized our imaginations for years, it seemed. While the vaccine saved us from the disease, it was the retelling of our quarantine story that redeemed us from spiritual paralysis.

We warmed so many chilly mountain evenings with cabin tales by the fireplace that sometimes now I can't distinguish between my own recall of an event from a memory of it formed by family storytelling. At all of our large family gatherings—Sunday dinners, birthdays, holidays, and relatives' visits—our family raconteurs took center stage, with Pop and his sons all in starring roles. They told family legends, spun out tales about town characters, one-upped each other by cracking jokes about childhood pranks, revealed fools being separated from their money in business deals gone awry, reported the coining of hilarious spoonerisms, and recounted how somebody had murdered the king's English.

There was, for example, Leo Haber, the man who worked at Fike's Chevrolet, our family's business competitor located just a block from our place. When I knew Leo, he was sixtyish and looked through gold, wire-rimmed glasses from under the bill of a tight-fitting ball cap. What could be seen of his hair, when he lifted his cap to smooth it, was thin and gray. However, the stories I heard about Leo came from his younger, more boisterous days. Once when a car drifted up to the gas pumps, Leo walked to the driver's door only to see everyone in the car slumped over on the seats. Apparently, carbon monoxide fumes had overcome them. After calling for help, Leo excitedly reported the condition of the car's occupants to a group of bystanders: "They were all semi-unconscientious!"

Even if he was not well versed in the lingo, Leo apparently knew a multitude of Bible verses by heart. According to one of my uncles, he frequently harangued people, growing especially evangelical after he'd had a swig or two of white lightning. One night after having had a few too many drinks of homemade brew, as the story goes, Leo stopped at McCann's soda fountain shop on his way home. Toting a bottle of the concoction hidden in a paper bag under his arm, Leo began preaching loudly to the folks who were seated at the counter, innocently enjoying fruit pies, rich sundaes, and thick milkshakes. The more he got wound up about being a Lamb of Jesus, the more Leo jumped and spun around. Directly, the pressure blew the cork off his bottle, spraying his captive audience with alcoholic foam. The customers got steaming mad, but Leo ignored their complaints, crying over the loss of his precious drink.

In these family storytelling performances, precise timing, accurate language, and dramatic delivery were essential. Each of my forebears was a master of ceremony, delivering the punch line just so in a resonant, baritone voice. Of course, as good as one telling might be, an immediate retelling by someone else could be just as rollicking, this time with liberal use of poetic license in revising the facts of the case. Sometimes in hot weather, meals would be served on the cabin's back patio or on the front lawn, looking down on the lake. But mostly I remember sitting inside, elbow to elbow at the long picnic table, eating fresh sweet corn, tomatoes, and summer squash—and listening to family talk. Even later, long after the dishes had been done and we kids had returned from outside with jarfuls of lightning bugs, someone would light a crackling log fire in the fireplace and the adults would talk some more, till after we kids had been tucked in for the night. Sometimes a loud laugh would wake us and we'd sneak out to the top of the stairs to eavesdrop.

As I recall this period, I seemed wholly occupied by the people and activities at the lake. I was not much fazed by what snatches of news I had heard about domestic and international events, nor did I ponder much my dad's fate and my lot. At the cabin with our large family I felt secure, and hearing familiar stories always heightened that sense of belonging and being whole.

Time, of course, inexorably changed things. Older family members died; younger ones moved away. New family patterns evolved. Evening and Sunday afternoon TV played more and we heard fewer stories of the old days. And, eventually, the cabin was ours no longer. After owning it for about eight years, Uncle Tom sold it. Pop had recently died and Aunt Rose had entered a long period of recuperation from a car accident. The Tom

Wrights moved from the apartment in our family home at 201 to a house of their own, out Main Street at the north end of town. I don't remember missing the cabin right away. As teenagers, we were spending three weeks each summer in Boy Scout and church camps. Something called dating also complicated our lives considerably. Many years passed before I understood what our time at that cabin by the lake meant. I had taken for granted its luxury and beauty, as well as what it provided us: a pastoral sanctuary out of harm's way and away from the tedium of daily town life. There we grew up, regenerated by carefree play, schooled by nature, and nurtured by the storytelling of a large, loving family. The building may be lost to us, but that cabin of memories is ever present.

10

THE ONE WHO
CALLED ME BOLO

Masontown, Pennsylvania

I remember Uncle Tom as the quintessential performer, not just at the cabin, but in public. Once when I was a youngster of five or six, I went to see Uncle Tom and his fellow Rotarians put on a minstrel show for charity at the Liberty Theater uptown. Before the show, someone took me down into the dressing room under the stage. I'm sure my eyes were as wide as saucers when I entered the narrow room with its bank of bright lights above mirrors that ran along the entire wall. Men were seated in front of the mirrors at a long counter that was filled with jars of cold cream, boxes of facial tissue, ashtrays, soda bottles, drinking glasses, and tubes of greasepaint. Everybody was in high spirits, filling that little room with a constant buzz of chatter and laughter. Some men had pushed back from the counter and were puffing cigarettes and sipping drinks. When Uncle Tom hailed me, the men greeted me with cheers and handshakes, as if I were visiting royalty. They were wearing tuxedo pants and shirts. Some hadn't yet put on their bow ties, and their suspenders hung loose. All of them had paper towels stuffed in around their collars, since they were putting black greasepaint on their faces. Someone teased me and held out a gob on his fingers, saying that I needed some to take the shine off the end of my nose.

When the curtain went up, I was sitting on the front row. Since all of the men had black faces and wigs and were standing and singing, I couldn't pick out Uncle Tom until they sat down in a row of chairs and began talking. Even though they were speaking in an exaggerated Negro dialect, I recognized Uncle Tom's voice. He was sitting in the center seat and doing most of the talking, with everybody addressing him. Someone called him Mr. Interlocutor. He started the jokes by asking the other men questions. I didn't understand all of the jokes, but everybody else did. The men on stage laughed, slapped their knees, and elbowed one another. The people in the audience laughed, screamed, and clapped. What I liked about the show was the singing. I don't know if I had ever heard a tenor voice before, but I marveled at the sweet, high, clear sound of Cousin Bruce Sterling singing an Al Jolson tune. My favorite time of the night, however, was when my friend Tommy Pento's brother, Bob, sang "Ol' Man River." When Bob's second bass voice slowed and dropped down to the lowest notes on "ja-il," I got cold chills. Although I didn't understand the song's historical context at the time, I recognized the mournful delivery of a very sad, weary man's story. When Bob finished the last note, the theater was absolutely silent and I held my breath for a second until the place erupted with cheers and whistles.

Beneath all his bravado, Uncle Tom knew his share of sadness. Thomas Hoover Wright was born a couple of months prematurely, on May 4, 1909, in Ronco, Pennsylvania. His birth followed by two years the birth of Daniel Wright, who had died after only two days. Named after Pop's best friend and his bus-line business partner, Thomas A. Hoover, Uncle Tom had been a bit of a rascal as a youngster, got into his fair share of scrapes, and loved playing practical jokes. One summer day, so the story goes, Uncle Tom and his brothers were recoating the roof with tar, when a neighbor boy, Gerald Stillwell, and his parents came back from a family outing. Sporting a white linen suit, Gerald waved at Uncle Tom from across the street, whereupon Uncle Tom motioned for Gerald to climb up the ladder to the rooftop. While spreading tar with a mop, Uncle Tom engaged Gerald in casual conversation, deftly jerking the mop handle back quickly at the end of each stroke, imperceptibly flipping tiny drops of tar on Gerald's white suit. By the time Gerald realized what was happening, the suit was peppered with black specks from his feet to his waist.

Uncle Tom owned a goodly portion of the Wrights' stubborn streak. As a high schooler, he brooked no guff from anyone. In fact, some said that he sought out scores to settle in order to be seen as someone to respect. Suspended for fighting at school, he was told that in order to return he would have to bring his dad to a meeting with the principal. Too headstrong to seek forgiveness so that he could get back in, he asked his dad to send him away to a private school. In the military culture at Staunton Military Academy in Virginia, Uncle Tom was able to express his competitive drive in athletics and his combative spirit in martial activities. An acquaintance had preceded Uncle Tom to Staunton. Harry "Bud" Brady was the son of Dr. Harry Brady, whose large and prominent Irish Catholic family lived in Gray's Landing, just south of Masontown. The senior Brady had been a colonel in the Spanish-American War; Bud would also achieve that rank serving in World War II. As a teenager, Uncle Tom was more than a little acquainted with the Bradys, including one of the daughters, Rose. At Staunton Uncle Tom made great friendships among fellow classmates, with many of whom he would soon serve in the war. He was particularly proud to have been on the swim team with Barry Goldwater.

Following in a Wright brothers' tradition, Uncle Tom also drove cars underage and over the speed limit—and he often added a little element of the daredevil, as well. Even so, he survived his youthful accidents. But his fame as a survivor comes from a time when he was nearing adulthood and, dressed to the nines, he was tooling through the countryside in a new sedan, and came upon Ball Hill much sooner than he had expected. Ball Hill is a notorious place where the road goes straight down over a precipitous drop-off. Already over the ridge when he hit the brakes, Uncle Tom managed only to lock up the car's front wheels, thus launching it into a rear-end-over-front-end roll ("ass over tea cups," in Mom's words) all the way down the hill. When passersby came upon the scene, they found a demolished car with its driver walking about in shredded clothes ("not torn, mind you, but shredded"—Mom again). He was covered with grit and grime, and his hair was tousled, but he didn't have so much as a scratch on him.

Several years later Uncle Tom showed his skill at slower-speed derring-do in an incident on our block— with equally untoward, if not quite so destructive, results. Eddie Wells, Aunt Frankie's twin brother, was himself an inventor of zany stunts. Showing off his new little Nash Rambler one morning, Eddie drove up the sidewalk from our place to Fike's Chevrolet dealership, navigating the narrow space between two oak trees and the stone wall in front of Mrs. Vignali's house. Not to be outdone, Uncle Tom climbed into a new Chrysler Imperial—a considerably larger vehicle, to say the least—and proceeded to traverse the same path. When he couldn't pass between the tight space on his first attempt, he backed up a bit, turned the front wheels, and tried from a slightly different angle. Still no luck. Another backup. Wedged in even worse. Finally, he was so jammed into the space, he couldn't even open the car door and had to crawl out through the window. When Mrs. Vignali saw what looked to her like high jinks in her front yard, she shouted from her front door, "Call the cops. He's drunk!" Upset at losing the gambit to Eddie and embarrassed by our neighbor's calling attention to his plight, Uncle Tom fetched the men from the shop who lifted and laboriously turned the car with jacks, this way and that, until they freed it—unscratched—from its wood and rock snare.

Following his graduation from Staunton, Uncle Tom went into the automobile business with his dad, eventually switching products from Ford to Chrysler, Plymouth, De Soto, and Dodge cars, and International trucks. He dated and soon married Rose Brady. Throughout most of my childhood, Uncle Tom and Aunt Rose lived with their children, Tommy Dick and Rosemary, in the apartment opposite ours at 201. When he rejoined the military to do his share in the Second World War, Uncle Tom entered as a captain, using his business skills to serve in an ordnance division. Stationed at the huge United States Army General Depot in Southern England, he crossed into France on D-Day plus two. While he may not have fought in the front lines, as my dad and Uncle Ben did, Uncle Tom left his family and his job as tax collector (which Aunt Rose took up in his absence) so that he could work in the business and logistical end of the war effort. Helping to supply the troops with tons of munitions and food, he served till the war's end.

He often told stories about his war years, mostly tales about zany characters, odd circumstances, or his direct superior—a major from South Carolina, who had gentlemanly manners, an elegant southern speech pattern, a keen wit, and a ravaging thirst for bourbon. Then there was the story of meeting his brother Ben. One day in early January of 1945, when Uncle Tom was working in Paris, he received a telegram from Uncle Ben requesting that he be met on an evening train. This was good news, indeed, to be able to see his younger brother after years of serving in separate sites in the European theater. Driven in a Jeep from work, Uncle Tom greeted Uncle Ben warmly at the station and, although he was surprised to see Uncle Ben unshaven and wearing a filthy uniform and muddy boots, he thought it best not to mention it there. On the drive back, as they were making small talk, the driver asked Uncle Ben where he had been.

"Oh, a little town down the road, called Bastogne," Uncle Ben casually replied, knowing the response he was sure to draw.

"Bastogne!" shouted both the driver and Uncle Tom. Uncle Ben had just left the battlefield after surviving one of the most brutal and prolonged battles of the war: the siege of Bastogne, which his unit, the 101st Airborne Division, had heroically defended.

After the initial shock and after leveling a barrage of questions in the stopped Jeep, Uncle Tom had a good laugh at having been bested by his little brother. Directly, he took Uncle Ben to the showers, got him a clean uniform, and took him out to dinner at a fine Parisian restaurant—the beginning of a few well-earned days of R and R for Uncle Ben.

Back home after the war, Uncle Tom resumed his business, although it was slow going for some time till the factories started to produce more cars. Customers put their names and choices of vehicles on a numbered list that hung on the showroom wall. As a new car arrived, the customer at the top of the list had the option of buying it or waiting until another shipment came in. Business demand remained strong and eventually production caught up with it to fire the great economic boom of the fifties.

Since both of his brothers worked in other towns, Uncle Tom was the sole Wright businessman in Masontown and, following his father, he was active in civic and social affairs. He joined the Uniontown Elks, Valley Lodge 459, and the Rotarians, and, like Uncle Lloyd, he was a thirty-second-degree Mason, member of the Syria Mosque. Taking a page from his father's civic spiritedness, Uncle Tom turned over the dealership showroom for an antique show during the town's sesquicentennial celebration in the fall of 1948.

Uncle Tom belonged to a weekly poker club with most of the town's physicians and he and Aunt Rose kept an active social life, going to nightspots for dancing and dining, and frequently attending private parties of friends and customers. Among his customers who enjoyed sharing the good life and showing off his new-found wealth was a man I knew as 'Milio, short for Emilio. 'Milio came from the old country and quickly used his street savvy and ethnic connections to build a trucking firm, hauling coal for the largest mining concerns in the area. He purchased a fleet of International trucks from Uncle Tom and continued to add to it as his business grew. 'Milio and his wife threw lavish parties, especially for the holidays. I remember Uncle Tom describing the elaborate Christmas decorations at their home, including a Christmas tree with tinsel, brightly colored lights, and twenty-dollar bills pinned to the branches.

Uncle Tom and Aunt Rose's nights out never interfered with raising Tommy Dick and Rosemary. Just as for us McClelland kids, Grandma and others in the household watched after the youngsters whenever their parents went out. Rosemary reported never knowing a time when she was alone in the house. Because Tommy Dick and Rosemary were several years older than Mary Jane and me, we were in different peer groups. Nonetheless, when we were together at 201 or at the cabin, they always treated us so amiably. There must be anomalies in every family. In ours they were Tommy Dick and Rosemary. These two first cousins of ours pos-

sessed, inside and out, the sweetest dispositions of all
the Wrights, rivaling Uncle Ben in sensitivity and pure,
human kindness.

Uncle Tom exhibited moments of sensitivity, too.
Many years later after Uncle Tom had moved from 201
to his own house, he made it a point to visit with
Grandma every day. He'd call up the stairs to her in
Welsh, asking how she was. She would shout back in
Welsh from wherever she was and hurry to the head of
the stairs, where they'd exchange pleasantries. This was
the family tongue, bits of which the Wright children had
learned when they overheard Grandma speaking with
her mother or one of her sisters. I'll always recall the
way Uncle Tom used that unique bond between him
and his mother, in good times and in bad, to hark back
to their common heritage, to evoke the family love that
bound them together.

Nobody enjoyed giving more than Uncle Tom did.
An animal lover like his dad, he had a horse and pet
dogs. When Rosemary was a preteen, he gave her twin
cocker spaniels. She easily came up with the name Boots
for the black one with white on his legs, but was
stumped trying to name the white one with several
large black spots. Aunt Rose reminded Rosemary that

when her grandad Brady forgot someone's name, he used to say, "Oh, Nicodemus." And so, Nicodemus he became. I remember the night that Uncle Tom and Rosemary groomed Boots and took him on a leash to the dog show at the football field. Nicky whimpered when he was left alone in the yard until they returned.

Christmastime in the family business was always a festive occasion, with decorations throughout the showroom and office. And Uncle Tom was always generous. On Christmas Eve day he gave each employee a ham or a turkey. Aunt Rose drove a car all day, delivering food baskets made at Vignali's grocery store to needy families in the poorer areas: under the bridge along the river at Mt. Sterling, along the run-down streetcar line, and in the outlying "patches," little communities near the worked-out mines and desolate coke fields.

Uncle Tom enjoyed teasing and joking with us. Once he marched us kids a block through our side alley to the jail, which we referred to as the lockup. He and one of the policemen put us in a cell, turned the key, and left us behind bars. We could tell by the exaggerated way they were talking about locking us up for the night that they were just kidding. We all had a good laugh when we walked back home. We couldn't wait to tell Mom that we had been in jail.

Then there was the time when we were in our early teens and Uncle Tom wished he could have jailed us. Pete and Teddy Dailey climbed into Mom's new station wagon while it was parked in the grease rack stall that Uncle Tom had put in the garage at 201. Teddy got behind the wheel and started it up. This 1957 Plymouth featured a push-button automatic drive. Teddy began punching the buttons, and, just as he pushed "R," he hit the gas, propelling the car into—and partway through—the sliding door. There was plenty of hell to pay for that misdeed. Mom was mad at Pete. Pete was mad at Teddy. Uncle Ted was mad at both of the boys. And Uncle Tom was mad at everybody. Uncle Ted insisted on helping to pay for the repairs, but Uncle Tom adamantly refused. Weeks later when Uncle Tom received a check in the mail, he made a big deal of tearing it up in front of us, making the point that we didn't need Dailey money to take care of our affairs.

Nearest in age among the Wright children, Uncle Tom and Mom had a close, and sometimes rocky, relationship. She complained that he taunted her as a girl. At the dinner table he furtively snatched up slice after slice of bread that she had just buttered and set on her plate, reducing her to tears. She always sought refuge in Pop. In adulthood, these siblings had words, too, such as those over the quarantine incident at the cabin. Another time, when Uncle Tom and Aunt Rose were putting on a new car showing down in the showroom, we three kids went tearing up and down the long hallway in a boisterous free-for-all, while Mom was out and Grandma was out of earshot. Uncle Tom came upstairs and locked us in the front pantry, telling us to hush until his show was over. Being locked in the large and well-lighted pantry was not exactly like imprisonment in the Tower of London. We contented ourselves until Mom returned. She, however, blew a gasket. Incensed over the situation, Mom immediately made plans to rent a small house on Washington Street from Lizzie Martin, a kindly Welsh lady and long-time friend of the family. Grandma was devastated at the prospect of us leaving the 201 household. In tears, she beseeched Pop, "Please talk to her, Dick." Knowing how to approach Mom in her agitated state, Pop let her blow off steam about her brother's bully tactics and about how she wasn't going to stay another day under the same roof. Finally, the storm of recrimination abated and Mom relented when Pop said, "Marianna, it would break your mother's heart." The next day—just like the days after all such family conflicts—everyone acted civilly, as if the incident had never occurred. At a safe distance in time and emotion, the incident was comically rendered at the dinner table and added to the family's repository of tales.

Anytime someone tooted his own horn or sounded a bit too self-righteous, Uncle Tom chanted a cute little ditty to bring him or her back to earth:

> *We don't smoke and*
> *We don't chew, and*
> *We don't go with girls that do.*
> *Our class won the Bible!*

He also had a nickname for just about everybody, including Mom, whom he pegged "Looper," a moniker from way back in childhood. Occasionally, he even called Grandma warmly by her shortened first name, "Deb." Pete he called "Peesda" and Mary Jane was "Katrina." (This rivalled Uncle Lloyd's calling her "Susie Yakatanksi," when he jokingly contended that she was not really a member of the family, but a poor baby in the hospital on whom Mom took pity, adopted, and brought home with me.) Uncle Tom's the one who called me "Bolo," a nickname that stuck only so long as he kept it uppermost in people's minds, and he tried his best to do so. Bolo was a clown's name and, as a pudgy-faced infant, I put Uncle Tom in mind of that circus performer.

One Memorial Day I recall being humiliated when Uncle Tom called me by my nickname. It wasn't his using the moniker "Bolo" that bothered me, in this case; it was the duty to which he called me. Veach Martin, the Chevrolet dealer and Uncle Tom's friend, had driven up in a new Corvette, explaining to Uncle Tom that he had no passengers for the parade, whereupon Uncle Tom turned to me and said, "C'mon, Bolo, get in and keep Veach company during the parade." I'm sure that Uncle Tom thought I would consider it a treat to ride in the parade, especially in the town's hottest new sports car. But I was so loyal to our family's Chrysler business that I felt mortified to be in the competition's car. I put my head down against the dashboard the whole way, looking up only occasionally to see how far we had progressed. Veach could see that I was embarrassed, but he thought I was simply crowd shy. He kept encouraging me, good-naturedly, to look up and wave to the bystanders. When he let me out after the parade, my back and legs were stiff from holding that posture so long. Climbing the stairs, I worried about how many people had recognized me riding in that damn Chevrolet.

The family's dicey economic plight in the decade before the war gave them all, Uncle Tom included, grave concerns about financial security. After a booming decade following the war, a downturn in the local economy, as well as one in Uncle Tom's health, presented him with difficult times in the last years of his life. I remember him and his faithful sales assistant, Nick Brolek, sitting through long late evenings, hoping customers would call. Uncle Tom went through a number of Pall Malls, while Nick nursed the same stogie all night, it seemed. In the end, my uncle, who had lived life at a fast pace, faced illness with the pluck you'd expect from a Wright, especially a feisty second son.

11

"LET'S GO TO THE CIRCUS!"

Masontown, Pennsylvania
Summer 1949–Winter 1950

When the circus came to town, it set up in the lot next to the fire hall, about two blocks away on Washington Street. In those days, although it served as a parking lot for Friday-night bingo games, it was not so much a lot as just a dusty field with scruffy tufts of grass sticking up between the stones. Since there was no fence, telephone poles lay around the circumference, permitting traffic to enter and exit only in designated areas. Every day that the circus was in town we enjoyed watching the elephants walk through the alley past our house, linked together trunk to tail, to get a drink of water. The big tent rose in the middle of the lot and smaller amusement tents and vendors' stands encircled it. At night it seemed a magical place with the strings of colored lights, the carousel music, the smells of roasted peanuts and cotton candy, and the noisy crowd. The clowns and acrobats, the jugglers and ladies on the trapeze, the magician and the lion tamer all looked so glamorous in their makeup and colorful, sequined outfits.

But in the daytime, when we sneaked over to the lot without Mom, the place looked desolate in the glare of the sun with all of the tent flaps tied down and the vendors' stands shuttered. The only people we saw then were old men with tattoos and grungy-looking teenagers wearing grimy T-shirts, shiny jeans, and clodhoppers. They all sat around on cable spools or upturned buckets, smoking cigarettes, looking at us with a kind of guardedness that you felt could turn mean in a minute.

Still, we loved the circus when the sun went down and we begged Mom to take us every night. One time I was so mesmerized by the sights that I tripped over a telephone pole at the lot's edge and a stone went through my lip. It took several stitches to close the wound, and I have worn a quarter-inch, half-moon-shaped scar under my lip ever since.

On Saturday mornings in winter, long after the circus days of summer, Mary Jane and I would reenact going to the circus with Mom. We'd climb in her bed, one on each side of her, hold her hands and close our eyes as Mom gave us a guided tour:

> "We're walking through the alley, going past the lockup. Hurry up, let's run, so whoever's in there won't see us.
>
> "Now we're coming to the Danielses' backyard. Say hello to everybody."
>
> We'd shout with her, "Hello, Maude. Hello, Fred. Hello, Delores. Hello, Freddie."
>
> "Okay, we're at the intersection at Washington Street. Look both ways. Any cars coming?"
>
> We'd shout, "No!"
>
> "Okay, then, let's cross. There's the Soxmans' house. Say hello to Mr. and Mrs. Soxman. Albert is not there anymore. He married an Australian woman he met in the war, and went home with her never to return. Can you imagine that, living on the other side of the world?"
>
> We'd shout, "No!"
>
> (When Mom said "in the war," I thought again about the brown boxes in her closet that held Dad's army stuff. I planned to sneak in there and look through it again when I found a chance.)

"And here are our cousins, the Lewis girls, on their porch. Let's wave and say hi."

Again, we'd join her in greeting them, "Hi, Deborah. Hi, Eleanor."

"There's Eben working in his shop at the back of the yard. Yell loud, so he'll hear us."

"Hi, Eben!" we'd scream.

"Over there are those so-and-sos. We don't speak to them anymore. Put your noses up in the air and walk right past them." We giggled as we stuck our noses up.

"Oh, hello, Tina! There's Tina Touscaris and her mother sweeping the sidewalk on the other side of the street. Wave." We'd drop Mom's hands long enough to wave broadly.

"Look over there. Good day, Mrs. Martin. We hope Marlene is feeling better.

"Here's the last house. See poor old George Snyder and his wife, Sarah. Smile and maybe he'll smile back. Let's say hello to Sarah." And so we did, cheering now because we had finally made it past all of the houses to the circus.

"Here we are, finally, at the circus!"

After taking us on imaginary rides and letting us eat nonexistent cotton candy, Mom asked if we were ready to go home, to which we screamed, "Yes!" Then, we'd gleefully retrace our phantasmagoric trip back home, eyes shut tight, with Mom guiding us each merry step of the way. If we could, we'd entice her to extend her make-believe spell just a little longer so we could do it all over again. Mom patiently—and every bit as enthusiastically—narrated a second fun-filled journey through our familiar neighborhood to the oh-so-distant circus wonderland.

12

A MOMENT'S RICHES

Masontown, Pennsylvania
April 1953

One Saturday morning a hard shaft of late April sun pierced through the TV glare in the living room at 201, luring us out onto the second-floor porch. The gray floorboards, the outdoor furniture, and the aluminum screens lay under a heavy winter sifting of black dust from the passing coal trucks. But the promise of spring drew us away from *Sky King* to a game of chase around the chaise lounge and the glider.

"Get in here before you look like you belong on the other side of the tracks with the Dotsons," Grandma barked. "June's coming to clean today, so I want you

Formal army portrait
of Lt. Ewing R. "Pete"
McClelland, ca. 1943

In my high school gradua-
tion portrait, taken in 1961,
at age seventeen, I bear a
close resemblance to Dad.

Dad and Mom on an outing
in the summer of their first
year of marriage, 1941

Dad, walking through
Sather Gate, the main
entrance to the University
of California-Berkeley
campus, ca. 1939

Our young family in the yard at 201, on Dad's last visit home before shipping out for the war in Europe in the summer of 1944. My brother Petie Dick is standing, Mom is holding Mary Jane, and Dad is holding me.

Mom, just before taking her new job as postmaster, ca. 1950

With his army unit, Dad is seated third from the right in the front row.

The newspaper article my brother and I came upon, discovering details about Dad's life and death, some of which were erroneous.

To Mrs. E. R. McClelland
201 N. Main, St.
Masontown, Penna.

From Lt E R McClelland
589 ... APO #443
% PM New York N.Y.
Sep 10 Dec 44

Dear Marianna,

Your breath will be coming in short pants after you read these next few lines. To begin with, my hands are quite cold consequently, this writing may not be too legible.

I have been to France and while there I had the opportunity to visit Le Havre + Rouen also quite a few others too insignificant to mention. The French certainly show the strain of war. Most everyone try to beg your rations. Cigarettes, candy + gum top the list.

At the present time I'm in Belgium. My impression is that they want to remain Belgians, but they are sympathetic to the Germans. They dislike Hitler.

We are situated in a wooded area which gives us a lot of protection from air observation. There is also a foot of snow which helps camouflage. I don't mind the cold too much. I have a good sleeping bag + several blankets. I would welcome a muffler + a pair of leather lined mittens. I'll write Pete ... a letter in a few days. I don't know when I'll get to see Tom, Ben ...

Handwritten V-mail letter from Dad

The last handwritten V-mail letter from Dad. The first portion is addressed to Pete and the second to Mom.

Telegram notifying Mom of Dad's death

Pop, ca. 1925, tuning up the engine of the Lincoln Touring
Car, which the Wright family used for its outings, including
frequent trips Up East to visit relatives.

We referred to the building at 201 North Main Street, Masontown, Pennsylvania, as "201" (pronounced "two-oh-one"). The family business, Wright Motor Company, was located on the first floor. The center door led upstairs to our home on the second floor. Taken about 1916, this picture shows Pop's employees, Gordon Wright, Sief Bowers, and Nick Brolek, in front of the showroom window.

On August 20, 1911, the family posed in front of Wright's general store in the coal patch in Ronco, Pennsylvania. From left, the family rooster perched on the Ford's windshield, Uncle Bill Lewis, Cousin Deborah Lewis, Pop, Grandma, Uncle Tom, and Gram. Uncle Lloyd is mounted on horseback.

A Wright family portrait taken in the living room at 201, ca. 1950. From left, seated: Grandma, Mom, Uncle Ben, and Pop; standing: Uncle Tom and Uncle Lloyd.

Mary Jane, Petie Dick, and me with pups in the yard at 201, ca. 1946

An informal portrait of Pop and us grandchildren, no doubt arranged and photographed by Uncle Lloyd, ca. 1949. Clockwise from the left: Rosemary, me, Tommy Dick, Petie Dick, and Mary Jane.

Entering the service as a sergeant, Uncle Ben later received a battlefield commission with promotion to 1st Lieutenant. In an army portrait taken at the Villore Studios in Rome, Italy, ca. 1943, Lt. Ben F. Wright proudly displays his new rank.

Uncle Ben with us twins playfully posed in Mary Jane's baby doll stroller in front of 201, ca. 1948

Uncle Lloyd rows us on the lake near the Soxman's cabin at Lake o' the Woods, West Virginia, ca. 1945, prior to the building of the Wright's cabin next door. From left, Rosemary, Petie Dick, Uncle Lloyd, and Mary Jane and me in our nanny Ella Spagin's lap.

Grandma McClelland with a large straw basket over her arm on Easter Sunday, 1976

My dog Pepper seated on the grand piano bench at 201, ca. 1960. Long unused, the piano holds a tinted portrait of Rosemary and Tommy Dick and a rack of 45 rpm records.

My class picture at fourteen, ca. 1958

My niece Amy and I visiting Dad's grave near Margarten, the Netherlands, July 2000

The cross marking Dad's grave at the American Military Cemetery at Margarten, the Netherlands. My brother, Pete, took this picture on his visit to the gravesite, ca. 1985.

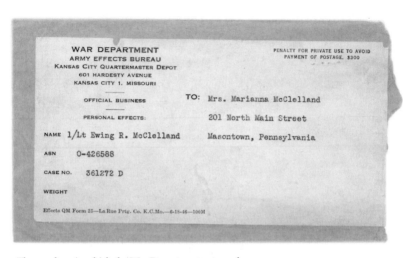

WAR DEPARTMENT
ARMY EFFECTS BUREAU
KANSAS CITY QUARTERMASTER DEPOT
601 HARDESTY AVENUE
KANSAS CITY 1, MISSOURI

PENALTY FOR PRIVATE USE TO AVOID
PAYMENT OF POSTAGE, $300

OFFICIAL BUSINESS

TO: Mrs. Marianna McClelland

PERSONAL EFFECTS:

201 North Main Street

NAME 1/Lt Ewing R. McClelland

Masontown, Pennsylvania

ASN   O-426588

CASE NO.   361272 D

WEIGHT

Effects QM Form 25—La Rue Prtg. Co. K.C.Mo.—6-18-46—100M

The envelope in which the War Department returned
to Mom the wedding ring she had given Dad

The wedding ring Mom had given Dad, returned to
her in protective packaging by the War Department

three outdoors till I call you for lunch. And take Pepper, too; she'll just be underfoot in here."

My brother won the race to the playhouse that Saturday morning and, as usual, my sister came in a tearful third: "I'm telling on you, Benny! You pushed me! I'm telling!" I placated her by telling her she could be in charge of spring cleaning in the playhouse. We hadn't been out in it since last Halloween when we hid in it after soaping Mr. Vignali's car windows. It was part of our vendetta. Why couldn't we erect a basketball hoop on our fence? He complained that we'd throw the ball over the fence into his flower garden. Why couldn't we bring some of Cousin Eben's rabbits to our place to raise? Because Old Man Vignali's cats would pester them to death. He forbade us to climb his grape arbor and flew into a rage when he caught my brother snipping off a bunch of plump red grapes that were destined for his winepress. He'd rather let the bees hollow out the brown-skinned pears that dropped from his large tree than let one of us eat them. When we griped about these injustices at home, Grandma always took his side.

"Listen, you smart alecks, that man came here all the way from Italy at sixteen. He hardly spoke a word of

English. He's worked all his life building the grocery business and has brought three sons into it. He deserves better than being hounded by the likes of you."

"Yeah, well, when Billy was over there last, he told us that we were all going to hell, because we didn't go to church."

"Now you listen to me. Never use that word around me again or I'll wash your mouth out with soap."

"But, Grandma, that's just what he said. I told him, 'We do, too, go to church!' 'But not the Catholic Church, so you're going to hell,' he repeated. 'Father and the nuns all told us that.'"

Grandma drew herself up and, putting her hands in her apron pockets, she turned squarely to us. "You never mind what Billy says. And you don't have to repeat a bad word just because he says it. Someday you'll understand. Nobody around here is going down below. And you boys are to stay out from under that man's feet, do you hear me!"

We reluctantly nodded our heads. The old man's grandson was a lonely only child. Was it a pure mean streak that made him throw the kittens against the garage doors, bashing their skulls? Or was it just desperate, forlornness gone wrong? Did he really believe the going-to-hell business or did he feign a superior position to cover some deep insecurity? Whatever the answers, the results were the same: one obnoxious, disconcerting act after another. And the old man's stooped figure seemed the devil incarnate to us, as horrible as the foul smell from his crooked black cigars that looked like gnarled twigs. So, at Halloween we soaped his windows and committed another act of daring piracy. Thinking that he valued the buckeyes that fell from his trees in prickly hulls, we sneaked out at night, Boy Scout flashlights in hand, scooped up nearly a bushel of them, and cached them under our playhouse trapdoor. He seemed not to notice they were missing.

That April morning those buckeyes confronted us as soon as we pried open the waterlogged trapdoor. They had sprouted and pushed yellow-green heads on spindly stems toward the sunlight that streamed in under the eaves. We quickly set to planting them around the playhouse to ensure an endless supply of our own buckeyes. Late that afternoon when we saw our wilted transplants bow their dried heads in the bright afternoon sun, we agreed that Mr. Vignali must've poured a caustic potion over them while we lunched. One of his cats leaped in through the open window of the play-house as we were plotting revenge.

"Let's put him in Mr. Vignali's new garbage can, the one with a lid," my brother suggested.

"No!" my sister gasped. "He'll smother."

"No, he won't," I retorted. "The Dotsons will be coming by before five and let him out."

Still, she refused to join in the caper and she was going to tell on us, until we prevailed upon her to stay in the playhouse and keep an eye on the Vignalis' back door. My brother stowed the cat under his sweatshirt and we made a beeline down the fencerow to the garbage cans. When we reached the end of the fence, we crouched behind the rusty, fifty-five-gallon drums in which we dumped our refuse. Just then a dull yellow slip of paper sailed into the weeds at my right elbow. As I reached for it, I noticed several others of different colors spread around the perimeter of the cans. Others caught my brother's eyes as they rode a gust of wind out of the can and swirled to a rustling halt at his feet. In a minute he and I clutched dozens in our fists. Dumb-founded by our discovery, we gathered in these strange-looking dollars in silence. The cat slipped away, unno-ticed and forgotten. We picked our way to the source of the windblown treasure, a crease-worn shopping bag that also contained gold breast pins, ribbons, a green cigarette lighter, a canteen, a brown cravat with a gold tie clasp attached—and several more bills.

We were dividing the booty when the Dotsons' truck rounded the corner into our back alley. We bounded over the fence and slipped into Mr. Vignali's garage. The truck groaned to a halt and idled roughly as a large black man jumped down from the trash-filled bed. He was a tall, angular man with a slack jaw; his parents had named him Tommy, but since he had a speech impediment and said Yommy, that was the name by which we all knew him. He possessed more strength than his hulk suggested. He grasped the rusty drums, one at a time, jerked them to his knee and heaved them over his shoulder into the truck bed, where a shorter, stouter look-alike emptied them and bounced them back beside the fence. Next they emptied the trash from Mr. Vignali's new, galvanized cans, baptizing them with a few well-placed dents. Then, Yommy mounted the garbage heap in the truck bed and the two rode on to the next stop, inured to their putrid-smelling perch.

My brother and I squatted in the damp garage, counting out equal amounts of the loot, like bank robbers splitting the take. Dazed by our good fortune, we could only giggle. Only occasionally did we glance at each other, so engrossed were we by these foreign-looking dollars. We didn't know what kind of money it was, but we were sure it wasn't play money. It was old and had a used look. Plus, the feel of the paper, the official symbols, the colors of ink—everything—said that this was the real thing. Suddenly, we heard his gruff voice.

"Those damn niggers!" he cursed repeatedly through teeth clenched onto a black, twiggy cigar. It was Mr. Vignali kicking the inside of one can to pop out a dent. My brother and I crammed all the loot we could into our pockets, rolled up the bag, and peeked out the door. Our trusty lookout was silhouetted in the playhouse window across the yard. Her terror-struck face was open-mouthed but frozen in silence. Before we could make a run for it, the old man pushed the can through the doorway and caught sight of us.

"Now, what you boys up to in here, eh?" he growled in broken English, emitting measured puffs of smoke with each word. Then we heard our sister clambering toward the house, wailing in fear. The old man hauled us into our yard by the scruffs of our necks, as he often toted his cats. Having heard the commotion, Uncle Tom came out of the shop to see what was the matter.

The old man turned us over to him with the satisfaction that justice would be meted out. Handing him the begrimed bag, the old man said, "Here, Tom. They claim they fished it out of the garbage. Their pockets are full of it, too. It's from the old country, lira, and francs, too."

"My God! Rose has thrown out my war souvenirs. Before you know it, my uniform will be next." He thanked the old man and led us into his office. He was so relieved that we had kept his wartime memorabilia from the dust heap that he rewarded each of us with a quarter—even my sister. My brother and I felt keenly the injustice of this. Little snitch sister gets a quarter, too. And what small potatoes the familiar coins were compared to exotic bills we had had for a moment. The old man had stripped us of yet another good thing.

Lord knows how many more vendettas we swore against him after that. But I don't recall making good on any of them. Childhood resolve has a way of unraveling. We were easily distracted. But the memory stays fixed of the old man as a spoiler.

13

POP

Masontown, Pennsylvania
December 1954

We kids loved to hear stories about Mom's childhood, so we always encouraged her to tell us some, like the first time she saw one of the old town characters. Once when she was a little girl going for a walk uptown with Pop, she spotted Ephraim Walters III, whose family's story was tied in with the region's pioneer history, his great-grandfather having been kidnapped and raised by the local Indian chiefs Yougashaw and Cornstalk. No matter what romantic history might be in this man's past, it was his present visage that undid Mom. Taking his customary walk from his home in the LeRoy Hotel on Main Street, Mr. Walters was dressed to the nines: fedora hat, black suit, and white shirt and black tie. But he looked especially owlish, wearing round, black-rimmed spectacles, chewing on a large cigar, and sporting a very long white beard. Shrieking, Mom jumped up and clung to Pop, with her arms and legs wrapped around him and her head buried in his chest. Pop spoke gently to her, as he tried to pry her loose. "Now, now. There's nothing to be scared of. That man is somebody's papa just like I am yours."

From the safety of Pop's arms, Mom peeked at the strange-looking man and asked, "Then, why don't they have a boy papa like me?"

We all laughed and when it died down, one of us repeated "boy papa" and we started laughing all over again.

Mom's papa kept close watch over her life, always providing her with a home and helping her advance professionally. In 1954, when Pop took to his bed and was sick for a long time, we knew that we had lost the head of our household. We kids had to be quiet when we went back by his bedroom. No running down the hall was permitted. We watched Grandma take in his medicine and heard her talking in a low voice with him. Early one morning, Mom called us to her bed and broke the news to us: "Pop died in his sleep last night." We joined her in a tearful moment during which we talked about Pop and how we would miss him. I remember asking for a memento. "Could I have one of his fishing poles?"

Mom apparently felt that I had gone overboard with sentimentality. She stopped sniffling and said tersely, "Oh, shut up and stop being so silly."

Pop's funeral was a big affair. Like a stone dropped into the water, Pop's death rippled through wide circles of people. He was not only the dominant force in our family but was also one of the town's leaders for half a century (its longest-serving borough president), and he was an influential political presence in the region. As we waited in the living room, everyone was somber. When people talked, they stood close to each other and spoke softly. We couldn't tell what they said. Uncle Lloyd came into the living room, red-eyed and sniffling. It was the first time I could recall seeing him teary-eyed. We had been dressed in our Sunday clothes for nearly an hour.

Mom had threatened us within an inch of our lives that we were not to get dirty before the service. Finally, it was time to go.

Just eleven years old when he died, I learned bits and pieces about Pop's life by listening to years of family stories. Born Richard Keating Wright in Plymouth, Pennsylvania, on October 8, 1879, my maternal grandfather was a man of many names: called "Dick" as a youngster, he was known to all his business associates in adulthood by his first two initials, "R. K." His wife fondly called him by his childhood moniker, as did his mother-in-law. His sons called him "Pa," and we grandchildren called him "Pop." Whatever the name, he was a man to be reckoned with. All of us revered him and none of us wanted to cross him. In tribute to him, Uncle Tom and Aunt Rose named their son Thomas Richard, who was called Tommy Dick. Likewise, Mom and Dad named their first child Ewing Richard, who was called Petie Dick.

When Pop was about five, living in Lucerne County, his mother died, leaving four young children, each of whom was sent to a different relative's home. Pop was raised by his maternal aunt and her husband, Lou Wagener. Pop's sister, Mary, was sent to relatives in

Cleveland, Ohio, and his brothers, James and Bill, went to other homes in central Pennsylvania. The Wageners adopted Pop without complaint, especially since Pop's father, old Benjamin Franklin Wright, had served a second term of enlistment in the Civil War, so that Lou could stay at home. That second tour of duty was a highly prized sacrifice and one long revered by the family, who treated Old Ben respectfully. His discharge paper, the evidence of his sacrifice, was also treated reverentially. An ornately printed document, the discharge paper bears an imprint of a bald eagle, with arrows in one talon and an olive branch in the other, standing on a shield, surrounded by three United States flags and encircled by a bevy of stars. The paper, with all of the pertinent information written in the swirling calligraphy of the 1860s, was handed down for generations, going to Old Ben's namesake grandson, my uncle Ben, and lastly on to his heirs.

Even though the Wageners took Pop in, he still had to earn his keep. Starting out as a youngster picking slag from the coal as it came down the conveyer belt off the tipple, he graduated at nine years of age to being a breaker boy, controlling the bucket that went deep down into the mine full of men and came back up full of coal.

When he received his weekly pay, he always hoped there would be a lot of coins. He had to give the dollar bills to the Wageners; he got to keep all the loose change. Throughout this period he attended school at night. After graduating from high school, he decided to move to the burgeoning coal fields in the southwestern part of the state. When Pop asked one of his cousins if he'd like to head south, too, he replied, "I'll stay here in the land of milk and honey." Pop replied without missing a beat, "Okay, but I'm headed to the land of smoke and money." First landing in Pittsburgh, he attended barber school to have a trade he could rely on when needed.

When Pop's father, Old Ben, a rigger, relocated from oil well drilling in Texas to Edenborn, Pennsylvania, to sink a coal mine shaft, Pop joined him. When Old Ben began building the structures that supported the new mine shafts, people in the region came from all around to see how it was done, especially erecting the tall towers that were made of heavy beams. Having constructed a tower that was lying on its side on the ground, Old Ben then sent word to local farmers, asking that they bring their teams of mules and horses to the site on a certain Saturday morning. When they arrived, so did a crowd of folks, curious to see what was going on. Old Ben hitched teams here and there along both sides of the structure, joining each with a different length of hoisting line. When he gave the signal, all of the teams pulled in unison and the tower rose into position.

Paying each farmer a good day's wage for just a morning's work, Old Ben became popular. He could count on someone offering him a drink wherever he went, though they say he never needed much encouragement to quaff some suds. In fact, one of my aunts called him a mean drunk.

Pop became a master mechanic and, later, an assistant superintendent in charge of the mine's machine shop. By now, he had also taught himself engineering. (As youngsters, we saw the dusty books on the attic shelves at 201. Uncle Lloyd proudly pointed them out to Pete, leafing through them to show Pete the chapter titles and the illustrations.) During a period of union organizing, when Pop was managing the machine shop at Frick's Ronco mine, he refused an order to carry a gun, saying that he didn't need it. Years later he explained to the family, "I told the men in the office that I knew my men and that most of the unionizers were my friends and neighbors. I wouldn't have any trouble.

They said to wear the gun or quit. So, I told them where to stick the gun and their job."

Leaving the mine, Pop began his own business, which had been a longtime goal. In the little coal patch of Ronco he opened a general store with a barber's chair and, in the rear, a poolroom. Grandma helped Pop run the store, which competed well against the mine's company store, especially since Pop opened the store on Sundays. Although he was regularly cited for breaking the local blue laws, he made such a good profit on Sundays that he gladly went to the courthouse in Uniontown each Monday morning to pay his one-dollar fine.

Pop and Grandma both maintained close ties with the family Up East, the area around Scranton, Pennsylvania. Pop also kept in touch with a childhood friend, a Mr. James, a rising political star who eventually became governor of the state. After one visit Up East, Pop drove back the first Ford car in Fayette County. In time, he ran a taxi business, for which he kept meticulous records. I remember seeing an old ledger with his handwritten entries for every trip that he made, including the date, destination, number of passengers, and the rate collected. Usually he recorded the passengers' names; if he didn't know them, he identified them by race or ethnic

origin in the WASP vernacular of the day: "Took a nig-
ger and two hunkies to Masontown."

Pop's racial views were what you would expect from
someone of his origin at the turn of the twentieth century in America: the garden-variety prejudice against
Catholics, Jews, Negroes, and southern and eastern
Europeans, who were also, of course, usually Catholic.
However, Pop was a reasonable, fair man who possessed
a great deal of civic spirit. He disliked anyone who harbored passionate racial hatred or held a vigilante men-
tality. In an incident with some new friends Pop showed
his true colors. According to a story I was told, Frank
and Josie Martin, a popular young couple from prominent families, lived on a large farm that sat atop a ridge
between Masontown and Ronco. Josie had attended
Waynesburg College, receiving a degree in music, the
only curriculum available to women then. Grandma
was proud to have made friends with a college-educated
woman, and Josie was so sweet-natured. During mid-
summer, the Martins invited Pop and Grandma to a
large gathering for a picnic dinner after church. Near
sundown, after eating a large, delightful meal and visiting with lots of new folks, Pop and Grandma noticed a
number of the men leaving the group and strolling

down a ravine behind the house. According to the story, as dark fell, a band of figures robed in Ku Klux Klan regalia paraded up out of the ravine, burned a cross, and performed a ceremony. As the hooded band marched back into the ravine, Pop suggested that he and Grandma say their good-byes and leave. On the way home, Pop was silent. Grandma, who had been so hopeful of forming a close friendship with Josie, feared that she could read Pop's mind. Finally, she asked, "How did you like the picnic, Dick?"

"We won't be going back" was his curt reply.

We kids never knew about this story when we attended Sunday school with the Martins' grandson, or when we rode horses on the farm. The still-attractive, white-haired grandparents had fine manners and were hospitable to us. But we never did see them among our family's friends.

Prejudice wasn't solely a Waspish trait, we knew. Our Roman Catholic friends acknowledged virulent anti-Protestant feeling, especially engendered during Father Kolb's reign at All Saints Church and School. When we walked to our respective schools—which were catty-corner from each other at the intersection of Church and Washington streets—the Catholic students stopped talking to us and crossed the street a block before they reached their school. They had been instructed not to speak to us and would get into big trouble if a nun or priest saw them break the rule. The Catholic students who attended our public school, like our cousin Rosemary, were forbidden to attend baccalaureate services whenever they were held in a Protestant church. We got a lot of our inside information from a number of Italian-American families who left the Catholic Church to join Protestant ones after Father Kolb offended them. The opinionated northern European did not hide his contempt for those from the southern climes.

In time, Pop moved from the little coal patch at Ronco some ten miles to Masontown, which had brick-paved main streets. Using some of his savings and cashing in on his connections, Pop acquired a dealership to sell Ford cars, opening on October 20, 1910. The family lived for a few years in a small bungalow at the north end of Main Street. When his growing automobile business grew, he soon built the large, two-story, brick building at 201 North Main Street that I knew as home.

Both a bit of a showman and a genius at things mechanical, Pop used his business's large showroom window to display more than just Model Ts. Whether it was an elaborate ad for political candidates or a piece of his handiwork, Pop figured that attracting attention to his place was good for business. When the building of a toll bridge across the Monongahela River was undertaken in 1926, Pop boosted the idea by making a model of it. Using parts from his own stockroom, he designed and built a six-foot replica of the bridge and set it up in his showroom window. A photograph of the display shows the bridge in operation with replicas of three cars, an electrical trolley car, a steam tractor, and three pedestrians (each with a dog) in passage. Other miniature supplements include a tollbooth, a traffic sign, signal lights, trees, banks, a sandy river bottom, and water. On the right side of the display Pop set up an expertly hand-lettered sign:

> MASONTOWN BRIDGE
> Commissioner
> Architect
> Inspector R. K. WRIGHT
> Engineer

Builder
Electrician

Of course, Pop also took credit for having constructed his model within the limits of the materials available to him. Located to the left of the bridge, a block-lettered sign explained: BUILT ENTIRELY OF FORD PARTS TAKEN FROM OUR STOCK AND WILL BE PUT BACK IN STOCK. IN BUILDING THIS BRIDGE NO HOLES BORED, NO PARTS CUT OR BENT. The model was an illustration not only of Pop's mechanical ingenuity but also of his frugality—a trait that came in handy more than once.

Another of Pop's unique engineering designs was a fence separating our yard from the Vignalis'. He crafted it out of automobile radius rods welded to a base fashioned from truck frames. This attractive, one-of-a-kind fence exhibited form and function; it was found art before its time. With Grandma's lilac bushes, peonies, irises, daylilies, and other perennials, the yard was a charming place. However, during Mom's youth the most prominent feature—rather creature—of the yard was Pat, the Boston terrier that was Mom's childhood pet.

Showing that he had a way with animals as well as with mechanics, Pop had trained Pat to stay in the yard and she did so faithfully—no matter if anybody else was at home and no matter how people tried to coax her out. It became a challenge to relatives and neighbors to invei- gle Pat out of the yard, somehow. They never could.

Pop had always liked and worked around animals. He had, of course, used horses and mules in the mine and had kept horses for the family to ride in Ronco. And he had a number of family pets. Pat was the one about whom I had heard the most. But she apparently was not the most notorious, according to a story that my brother told me. When the family lived in Ronco, Pop had a pit bull, a champion fighter. Not only did Pop win a great deal of money wagering the dog against all comers, but he never worried about leaving the house and store unattended. He just chained the dog on the front porch.

An astute and industrious man, Pop was also known to mix it up with anyone who looked cross-eyed at him. Once when he had gone to the John Struble farm with a Model T, a tenant farmer named Dick started mouthing off at Pop about the tin lizzie he was driving. Pop got out of the car, ran up to the heckler, and directly beat him up. John Struble, a crude man who rode his horse bareback and enjoyed badgering people, saw Pop in town later and said, "Hey, Dick. I hear you licked our Dick." The play on words infuriated Pop, but he laid off old John, figuring he'd had enough of the Strubles and their ilk.

Pop continued to expand his business interests, establishing the town's first bus service in 1917, in partnership with William D. Lewis, his brother-in-law who also came from Up East, and with the financial backing of Thomas A. Hoover, his best friend. They began with a large, Dodge touring car for which they fabricated isinglass windows to protect passengers from wind and weather. While this public transportation was a boon to everyone in the region, nobody benefited from it more than Gram. No longer needing to find a ride from someone, she boarded the bus to make her rounds throughout the various little patches and hamlets. Because her son-in-law was an owner, Gram never paid the bus fare. After all, except for an occasional visit for tea with one of her Welsh compatriots, Gram's traveling involved medical, spiritual, or charitable work. When the bus line was sold, Gram continued to ride free, scoffing at any driver who asked her to drop the fare in the box. The new owner finally came to Pop, asking if he would please inform Mrs. Lloyd that she now had to pay for her rides. Taking a more prudent course, Pop said,

"Just let her ride. Keep track of her fares and send me a bill each month."

Pop was called on to show his mettle when the Great Depression hit and the local bank closed suddenly, in the spring of 1931. Without any warning from the bank president, his close friend, Pop lost everything except the business inventory that he had on hand and the food in the pantry. Moreover, as one of the bank's directors, he was responsible for making up its losses. Bill Graham, the bank president, called a meeting and informed each of the directors of his amount of the debt. At the close of the meeting, Graham, a confidant of Pop's, asked him to stay for a minute. When the room cleared, Graham said, "Dick, I can get you relieved from this debt."

"What about the others?" Pop inquired.

"I can only carry this for you, Dick. And I would really like to. Nobody needs to know about it."

"No thanks, Bill. Set up a loan for me and I'll pay it off like all the others."

Pop made payments on his debt for nearly two decades. At least one of his sons helped, too. During the war, Uncle Ben—who was still single—sent his monthly allotment home for Pop to pay on the loan. When Pop's children inherited the place at 201, after Pop and Grandma died, Uncle Lloyd willed his percentage of the ownership to Uncle Ben as repayment.

During the depression Pop also purchased items on the black market, finding for his wife and daughter even such scarce personal items as nylon stockings, shampoo, and fingernail polish. When Mom went off to nearby California State Teachers College of Pennsylvania in 1934, she had a generous supply of personal items. All of the girls used to flock to her room to borrow from her toiletries. They also admired her fine wardrobe, which consisted of several of Grandma's plentiful suits and dresses, altered to fit Mom.

Pop was proud that he was able to maintain his business and sustain his family throughout the depression without any government assistance. Interestingly, a once-onerous Ford Motor Company policy helped him survive the hard times. Each year the company required dealers to purchase a large inventory of parts, a lot more than they ever used. Ironically, that stockpile of parts became Pop's cash cow. Because people could not afford to buy new cars, they had to repair their old ones to keep them serviceable for a longer period of time. For years Pop kept the business afloat with the repair shop and parts store trade until car sales picked up again. He was also not above some histrionics to illustrate his plight. Once when Ford sent a representative to Pop's dealership to inquire as to why Pop was not acquiring merchandise on the scale that they required, Pop met him dressed in a pair of coveralls, making as though things were so dire that Pop had to work as a common mechanic, too. When he turned the business over to Uncle Tom after the war, the assets totaled well over a half million dollars.

Pop also helped others in their business dealings. Sometime in the late thirties, he found a nice little fishing establishment on Tilghman Island, Maryland, in the Chesapeake Bay. An ardent fisherman, Pop struck up a friendship with the owner, Captain Levin Harrison, and his father, old Captain Harrison. Levin Junior was more than ten years younger than Pop, and the senior had as much as ten years on Pop. Both had a lifelong knowledge about fishing the bay waters. Captain Levin and his wife, Miss Alice, had two boys and a girl. Miss Alice managed the hotel and dining room at the Chesapeake House where the food and hospitality were unparalleled. While the Wrights and the Harrisons came from two different worlds, they hit it off, developing deep friendships.

Today a seven-mile bridge serves to connect Tilghman Island with the mainland, but before the war the place was much less accessible. From western Pennsylvania it was a two-day journey. The Wrights traveled east across the state on the Pennsylvania Turnpike, making a stopover at a boardinghouse near Hagerstown, Maryland. The journey's second day involved more time than distance, requiring rides on two different ferries to reach the Chesapeake House. At Annapolis the first ferry departed for Tent Island, where—after quite a wait—the second boat departed for Tilghman Island.

While the Harrisons had a good business, it served mostly folks from the neighboring vicinity. Pop saw an opportunity to develop the business and applied his acumen to market the family's pleasure-fishing business. He took pictures of the Chesapeake House, of the *Lev-Ron-Son* with the captain and clients aboard, and of the wonderful catches they made. Returning home, Pop designed and wrote an advertising brochure. Printed on yellow, heavy stock paper, "Tilghman Fever" folded out into five panels with photos, descriptions of the place, rates, address, and phone number. Mailing these to all of his customers, business associates, political acquaintances, and friends, Pop created a boom for the Chesapeake House's business. Pop, Grandma, and their children became like family to the Harrisons, spending weeks at the island every summer. When the Wrights arrived in a brand-new 1940 Chrysler, it made quite an impression on six-year-old Buddy Harrison. New cars didn't show up on the island every day. Eventually, the Harrisons took their family vacations during part of the time that the Wrights came, trusting Pop to run the boats and Grandma to run the restaurant and house. During winter vacations the Harrisons visited Masontown, staying at 201 and making the rounds at the homes of the many customers from the region whom Pop had brought to them, including the Smiths, Larry McGee, and Phil Urbany. Buddy Harrison and Jim Smith, who are the same age, developed a fast friendship and visited each other numerous times over the years, even stirring up some mischief on the quiet island in their teen years.

Whenever the family traveled to the bay, they thought the more, the merrier. As a result, just about everyone in the extended family who enjoyed the water got to go along at some point. Even my dad vacationed with Mom and the family at the bay—something I never knew until recently, when I saw for the first time some photos of him there. Having never heard of him going to the bay, I assumed that he couldn't get leave from the army, but he did so, at least once.

When we kids were big enough, Mom took us along on these annual family outings to the bay. Mary Jane remembers Mom grabbing her arm when she nearly entered the wrong bathroom on the ferryboat. Mary Jane didn't know what "Colored Women" on the sign meant. We spotted jellyfish for the first time in the bay. They seemed so pretty, gracefully floating about. Then, we heard how badly we'd get stung if we touched them. Throughout my childhood and well into my teens—long after Pop's death—the Harrisons were still giving our family the red carpet treatment during our visits. They reserved a wing of the hotel for us and also a boat for our exclusive use. At mealtimes, they served our table family-style, with all of the items on the dining room menu. Mom's favorite was their special Maryland crab cakes. We bathed and dressed up for dinner each evening, which Petie, in particular, did not like to do.

Out on the water in the boat, we kids were a handful. Pete recalls being tied by his waist to the cabin, with just enough rope to reach the rail and cast his line out. When we got big enough, we took turns steering, taking the wheel from Captain Harrison or one of his sons, until we got to our fishing spot. Then, nobody wanted to be in the cabin, because we caught and reeled in fish as fast as we could get our lines in the water. We kept the fish iced down in large metal chests. (When we returned to Masontown, it seemed as if we gave away fish to friends and neighbors for a week or more. Pop drove a car around town, stopping in driveways, and we scooped the fish out of the tub in the trunk to give to folks. If some-one refused, Pop got back in the car and said, "Okay, cross her off the list." Next year, we wouldn't stop there.)

After a long day on the boat, we returned to the house and played cards or worked a jigsaw puzzle with the Harrisons' daughter, Sondra. Nightly, one of the kitchen helpers rode a bicycle to town and brought back scoops of ice cream in a pan on the handlebars. Dipping out into cups whatever variety we wanted, we ate the melting ice cream quickly.

I remember only sunny, breezy days on the water and hot sticky nights in the house. But Mom recalled bad weather, too. During her retirement, she once wrote about a scary experience: "One night while fishing on the Chesapeake Bay, a storm came up suddenly. The boat was tossing back and forth. I was sitting on the chest where the life jackets were kept. The Captain asked me to let him get something out of the chest. I felt faint. I thought he was going to give us life jackets. He just wanted his rain coat."

The relationship between the Wright and Harrison families began in the thirties and lasted for nearly three decades. Before Uncle Tom had the cabin built at Lake o' the Woods, this was the family's summer retreat—and its view into southern coastal culture. For us kids, it was a luxurious and exotic world, where people's speech, food, and customs were so different. The daily action on the boat and the evenings of lassitude seemed as if they would never end. But, of course, eventually they did. The annual visit to Tilghman Island was a special experience that we thoroughly enjoyed. We treasure even more our memories of it now that we no longer have it or the people with whom we shared it.

For most of his life Pop did all of the odd jobs around 201. Usually, he did fine work, but once he out-

foxed himself, as Grandma told us many years after the fact. Once when she told him that the runner of carpet down the length of the hall was worn and needed to be replaced, Pop thought he could fix it up himself and save some money. He told her that he had an idea. Going to work, he taped newspaper to protect the wood along each side of the runner and painted the carpet with dark blue Ford automotive paint, which he had in plentiful supply. As he worked, Grandma watched him without comment. When he finished the job late that night, he asked, "What do you think, Deb?" Sensing that it was not a good time to lodge a complaint, Grandma said simply, "Let's see what it looks like in the light tomorrow morning." When they looked at the carpet in daylight, Pop could tell from Grandma's face that it didn't meet with her approval. Still she held her tongue, knowing the value of silence. "Okay," he relented, "get your coat. We'll go to the carpet store."

Pop still did fine refinishing work when I was growing up. He refinished the wooden flooring on each side of the runner, using a steel comb and a rubber wood-grain tool to make it look like finely grained wood. He also painted the horsehair plaster walls a light neutral color; on the lower half he then used crumpled newspaper to overlay a dark brown pattern on it. Between the top and bottom halves he painted a dark brown stripe—perfectly level and with neat, straight edges—along the entire length of the walls.

An expert craftsman and a perfectionist, Pop worked intensely and expected any helper to be as proficient as he was. When Aunt Sally was assisting him in making a plumb line on a wallpapering job once, she didn't do it just as he wanted, and he barked, "Jesus Christ, Sarah, can't you even snap a chalk line!"

If he showed impatience with less able helpers, neither did Pop appreciate a jibe at his workmanship. Because Grandma disliked leaning down to load the dryer, Pop built a two-foot stand that put the door at chest height. Using six-by-six posts, he constucted a sturdy stand that would last a lifetime. Painting it high-gloss white with black trim around the base of the legs, he matched it with all of the white-enameled appliances: hot-water heater, washer, dryer, and sink. When Pop proudly showed off his handiwork to a visiting couple, the husband queried sarcastically, "R. K., do those legs go all the way down into the ground?" Peeved, Pop walked away.

Another time, he redid the bathroom in anticipation of Grandma's having her church circle meeting at the house. Using the trendy new plastic tiles of the fifties, he tiled halfway up the walls, and repapered the top half. The blue tiles had white swirls in them, looking much like cirrus clouds. Pop smartly trimmed the walls with a routed piece of wood painted in high-gloss black. Throughout the evening during the circle meeting, Pop sat reading in his bedroom—next to the bathroom—waiting with the door ajar to see anyone who passed to visit the toilet. The ladies had coffee or tea to begin with, conducted the evening's lesson, ate Grandma's prized apple crumb pie, chatted, and had more coffee and tea. As the ladies left, one by one, for home, Pop realized that nobody was going to visit the bathroom. Nobody was going to see his handiwork. When Grandma came to bed, Pop asked how the meeting went.

"Just fine."

"Not one good piss in the whole crowd," he muttered in disgust.

Of course, Pop was primed to dislike the church ladies. "Those belly Presbyterians," he called them derisively, because Grandma seemed to cook for and attend church dinners all the time. A personal experience also put an edge on his view of the faithful ladies. Not a devout man, Pop rarely attended church. Around election time, however, he always appeared on the pew where Grandma and the children regularly sat. Once he overheard someone whisper, "There's Dick Wright. Must be an election coming up." After leaving that day, he never walked through the church doors again, not wanting to be caught at that form of hypocrisy another time.

Pop had his share of sayings, such as his warning about not aiding or abetting anyone in doing anything stupid: "Never sell a German a rope on a rainy day." And whether Pop had prostate trouble himself, I don't know, but I recall him joking about it in a philosophical way: "A man spends the first half of his life trying to make money and the second half trying to make water." Besides being a storyteller, he was also a bit of a showman. As a young man, he played a trumpet, recording songs into the day's latest Edison recorder. In addition to doing some simple sleight-of-hand magic tricks, Pop also entertained the family by picking coins up from the floor with his toes. No doubt he was an admirer of the Great Houdini.

Pop's political career was based on his activities in the Republican Party at all levels. Through grassroots politicking, he earned spots for himself first on the school board and then on the borough council. He became the town's longest-serving borough member, and was for a lengthy stint its president. Working with Bill Lewis, he also established the local volunteer fire department, selling the town fire trucks at cost and donating land behind 201 for the municipal building, which housed the fire hall and the jail. At this time, when Pop served as borough president, Bill Lewis as burgess, and Bertie Hide as police chief, they were jokingly referred to as the Three Wise Men from the East, because all three had come from Up East.

Pop was instrumental in the constructing of the municipal building and the school building, both out of the same yellow brick. (I have always wondered what brickmaker friend gave Pop a good deal on all that brick.) He also figured prominently in brokering the deal to purchase a large tract of land for the high school football field, conveniently located just west of Washington Street, and oversaw the paving of most of the side streets in town. He had photographs of several street curbs and storm drains, neatly captioned in his handwriting and showing some of the municipal improvements made during his tenure on the borough.

Besides having the right pedigree, Pop took naturally to politics. He enjoyed the company of all sorts of people, had a forthright manner, was articulate, had an entertaining story for every occasion, and earnestly wanted to make the world a better place. Next to fishing, politics was Pop's favorite avocation. Grandma was used to him being gone lots of evenings to meetings, but she didn't like it when he stayed out past midnight. To her, that meant the business meeting had concluded and the drinking session had commenced. He brooked none of her watchfulness, however. If she were waiting up for him into the wee hours, he went on the offensive, scolding her for missing her sleep, with all that she would have to do the next day running the house.

Grandma eventually got the upper hand, however. On those mornings when he was hung over, Pop rose very late. Seating himself unsteadily at the breakfast table, he asked for a cup of Postum. Grandma, however, placed a large empty glass at his place.

POP   { 191 }

"Oh, Deb!" he protested weakly. Directly, she cracked two eggs on the rim of the glass and dropped them in. "Oh, no, Deb!" he said, objecting more loudly this time.

"Now, drink it," she ordered, "and I'll get your Postum."

Looking wan, Pop resignedly took his medicine. We kids never knew whether this raw-egg drink was administered as a medicinal tonic or as a punishment, but we suspected that Grandma took some satisfaction in serving it as both.

Pop attended the Republican National Convention as a delegate from Pennsylvania when Al Smith was nominated. While there, he suffered a heart attack that slowed him down for a time. Still an active pol when Ike was elected in 1951, Pop was given, through political patronage, the opportunity of naming a qualified individual to fill the county's postmaster position, which Gilmore Provins was vacating. Pop broached the subject to his family at dinner one Sunday, asking if any of his boys wanted the job. The three of them declined, each already being gainfully employed. After a moment of silence Mom suggested, somewhat timidly, that she'd leave her teaching position to take the job. Raucous laughter broke out around the table, angering her so that she spoke more insistently, demanding that she be taken seriously as a candidate.

"You have to pass a test, Marianna," Pop said, referring to the civil service examination.

Having done exceptional work all through school and college, Mom was supremely confident about her test-taking abilities and was more than a little piqued that her father might think that a test would be an impediment.

"I can pass a test!" she exclaimed in exasperation.

Her brothers laughed again, seeing their sister's dander up. However, sobered by her earnestness, Pop told her to take the exam and, if she qualified, he would recommend her. Among a large field of candidates, two others close to our family also vied for the job: first cousin Dan Lewis, a rural mail carrier, was Bill Lewis's son and a classmate and close friend of Mom's all through school. Bud Brady was Aunt Rose's brother. Both were veterans. Another first cousin and respected family member, Bruce Sterling, son of Pop's sister, Mary, served—and intended to continue serving—as assistant postmaster. Bruce felt he was in the hot seat from all directions during the appointment process.

However, besides her high score on the exam, Mom's candidacy had a great deal supporting it, especially her being a widow of a veteran. Also, Pop, who had contributed generously to the Republican Party and who still had a good friend in Governor James, had assurances that his recommendation would carry the day. Still, in his typical fashion, he crossed all the t's and dotted all the i's. Leaving nothing to chance, he lobbied for Mom at the top political levels. Dan and Bud, so it was said, worked feverishly at the grass roots. On March 17, 1953, the *Morning Herald* carried a banner above the masthead: "War Widow Is Named Postmistress At Masontown." The headline below the masthead read: "1,200 Candidates Listed." Accompanying the front-page story about Mom and her appointment to the prestigious position were three photos, all from our school portraits: a large one of Mom, one of Pete, and one of Mary Jane and me together. Within the article was a specific detail about Dad's death that I had never heard (and that also differed from the initial report that Mom had received in the notification telegram): "Mrs. McClelland is the mother of three children and the widow of Lieut. Ewing 'Patsy' McClelland, one of the heroes of the Battle of the Bulge in World War II. Lieut.

McClelland was a member of the 106th Infantry Division engaged in the famous Battle of Bastogne. It was after this battle the Germans lined-up and massacred more than 300 prisoners of war, one of whom was Lieut. McClelland."

There it was, supposedly factual: *massacred more than 300 prisoners of war, one of whom was Lieut. McClelland.* Was this a fact that had been uncovered in the years following the war? Or was this the creation of a news reporter or of one of Mom's zealous supporters? The article, of course, contains errors. At one point, Mom is referred to as Mrs. Provins. Where the nickname "Patsy" for my dad came from is anybody's guess. The massacre of Malmedy followed the Bulge, not Bastogne. Having been captured in the opening days of the Battle of the Bulge, Dad and his unit were not on the field to become engaged in the Battle of Bastogne. Later, too, historians corrected the number of prisoners killed, lowering it from three hundred to seventy-two. When I read the article, though, I wondered if Dad really was among those massacred. I also wondered if that was what Mom and the family believed. If so, perhaps that is why nobody ever mentioned much about Dad and his death. Such an awful fate!

The article went on to state that when other candidates learned that a war hero's widow had applied, all but a few voluntarily withdrew. That is probably accurate, but what is also undoubtedly true is that when they learned that the woman was R. K. Wright's daughter, they withdrew. Mom served in the position for twenty-five years—the longest tenure at that post—under a portrait of the benignly smiling Dwight David Eisenhower, whose signature appeared on a document authorizing her appointment. Bud Brady, ever good-humored and a gentleman, never revealed his disappointment. On the other hand, Dan Lewis blew a fuse, finding it so hard to lose to Mom. He held a noisy grudge for years—even as her employee, perhaps the hardest pill for him to swallow.

The final testimony to Pop's staying power in the state's Republican Party was that, after he retired from the automobile business and was in failing health, he was appointed to be a hearing inspector for the state traffic department and became Judge Wright. Most of my firsthand memories of Pop come from this period of time, when he was able to be home more. On the days that he went to court he breakfasted in the dining room dressed in a starched white shirt and tie. Taking his seat at the head of the table, he tucked a large linen napkin in his collar and partook of a full breakfast of orange juice, a soft-boiled egg (three minutes, not a second more), toast, and a cup of Postum. He lifted the egg from its porcelain holder, cracked it with a spoon, scooped out the insides into a small dish, and seasoned it heavily with salt and pepper. With each spoonful of egg, he took a bite of toast, which he had buttered generously and on which he had heaped spoonfuls of homemade jam. After eating, he browsed through the newspaper, while drinking a second cup of Postum. When his driver, Mr. Venturini, arrived, he and his court recorder, Mr. Olenik, left for work at the courthouse. When he returned, he often brought home amusing stories from the day's docket.

Once he regaled us with the story of a recent immigrant who was charged with a moving traffic violation. It was alleged that one foggy night the man rear-ended a car that was stopped in an intersection, waiting to make a left turn.

Judge Wright: "Sir, as you approached the intersection, did you see the vehicle stopped ahead of you?"

Defendant: "No, judge. I'm no see it." (Pop rendered the man's broken English with great relish.)

Judge Wright: "Well, as you approached the intersection, did you see the man holding out his left hand to signal that he was about to turn?"

Defendant (with respect, but with some exasperation at the judge, who asked such a silly question): "Judge, if no can see big car, how can see little hand?"

Pop enjoyed mimicking the man's way of talking, but in this tale, as in many others, he gave the man his due for being savvy. Enjoying the role of senior raconteur in the family, Pop always looked for new material from his daily experiences. On one of the Harrison family's visits during Pop's judgeship, he took young Buddy Harrison along to court for the day. As Captain Buddy reported it many years later, "After one case, Judge Wright returned to his chambers, chuckling and reaching for a pencil. Oh, that defendant gave a great excuse. I have to write that one down, so I won't forget it."

Judge Wright was also used to meting out punishment to any young offenders in his household. We McClellands were a rowdy crew and the hallway that ran the entire length of the house gave us plenty of runway to get up a lot of speed. When he had had enough, Pop reached for the heavy, wooden yardstick that hung on a nail on the kitchen wall and took out after us. Our best defense was to put the dining room table between him and us, circling around it and scooting underneath it when he approached. If we were lucky enough to wear him down, he would negotiate a compromise: "You fellows sit out on the porch for a spell, till I tell you to get up, and I won't spank you." Of course, we never would have gotten away with any such nonsense when he was in his prime, but we managed it when his health and will declined.

Pop's reputation as a civic leader never declined. He still commanded respect long after he ended his active career, as an incident with a shop owner proved. When Pete was about seven and we twins were not yet six, Mom went on vacation and gave each of us kids some spending money, three dollars apiece, which was quite a sum in those days. Pete talked Mary Jane and me out of our money and spent all of it on pocketknives uptown at John's Bus Stop. John's was a little seedy storefront where local buses stopped. Among John's wares were sodas, snacks, candy, and junk—assorted toys and penknives. In a corner there were some pinball machines. As Pete told the story, when he brought home a paper bag full of pocketknives, "Grandma and Pop were not as happy about the knives as I was." Pete ironically understated Pop's reaction. I'm sure he had a "conniption fit," as we used to say. Pop directly wrote a note to John and made Pete take it and the knives back to the Bus Stop. John returned the money and told Pete, "You never come in here again!" We never knew what Pop wrote in the note, but it must have scared John, who scared Pete. As Pete said, "It was years before I ever did go in there again."

Pop was also a big believer in preventing infections by putting iodine or Mercurochrome on cuts, insect bites, and bee stings. He knew how much we kids feared that burning stuff in the blue bottles, so when he applied it to a fresh scrape, he'd say, "Okay, now, run down the hall and come back and I'll put a Band-Aid on it." We'd run screaming down the hall and back. By then it would have stopped burning enough for him to put on a white adhesive bandage.

One of my most distinct memories during this period involves Pop and me in a battle of wills over a canary—*my* new canary. Mom, who had a special fondness for birds, had several canaries over the years. Once when I was rummaging through our pantry looking for a snack, I came upon a small, white Fannie Farmer candy box. It was very light and a bit dingy looking, but I thought it might still hold a piece of edible chocolate. Opening it, I gasped: there was a canary, eyes closed, belly up, feet tucked and claws curled. I ran to Mom and said, "Look!"

"He was one of my favorites," she said warmly, as if she were looking at a picture of an old beau. A special fondness, indeed. But why should I have been so startled about Mom's little feathered keepsake, when we men mount on living room walls, as trophies, the heads of dead animals for whom we have no particular affection?

Later, I benefited from Mom's fondness for canaries when she got me one for a present. We placed it in the old cage by the window near the dining room table. With the family gathered around, Mom and I whistled softly, looking into the cage, hoping to hear its first song. The cage hung from a round, metal hoop that had been placed in the stand of an old floor lamp. For a birdcage, it had quite an ornate base.

As the bird hopped from the near rung to the swing in the center and over to the far rung, Pop asked, "What are you going to call it?"

"Jerry," I said brightly.

"Jerry? That's a silly name for a bird."

"I like Jerry."

"Jerry is a little boy's name, not a bird's name. Let's call him Ike." Having made his way, Horatio Alger–like, in the rough-and-tumble world of American business in the first half of the century and hoping for a sustained period of peace after such horrific world wars, Pop harbored a devotion to the newly elected president that emanated from the heart of his Republican soul. And here was proof positive.

"No. It's Jerry."

"I say we name him Ike."

"No! I'm calling him Jerry!"

Walking away, Pop announced broadly, with finality, "His name is Ike."

At night we covered the birdcage to darken it, so that the bird could settle down and rest. Mom had had a brown cloth cover made with a metal handle fastened to its top and a pleated ruffle around its bottom. One day the cover disappeared. That night Pop came in with it and placed it over the birdcage. There, in bright brass letters he had had stitched to the center of the front, was the bird's name: IKE.

Adamantly sticking to my guns, I continued calling the bird Jerry. My sister contented herself with the amalgam Jerry-Ike, so as not to hurt anyone's feelings. From time to time, as family stories were traded, we'd recount the naming of my new canary and have a good laugh. Usually, someone would add a footnote about the trait of stubbornness that ran through the Wright clan, with Pop and me as its two current, but by no means sole, exemplars.

Oblivious to the name game, the canary sang cheerfully, becoming more robust and enthusiastic when people entered the room and whistled back to it. The bird remained for a long time part of the household, until its sudden demise after a fumigating serviceman visited the house. Mom wasn't to be without a canary for long, so another soon replaced it, but—with Pop and Jerry-Ike both gone from the scene and me away at school—there was no stir over its name, and no special fondness for the new warbler from anyone but Mom.

A large tree casts a big shadow. Pop possessed such ennobling personal traits—indomitable will, native intelligence, easy affability, and far-reaching vision in personal, business, and civic affairs—that he not only created early success, but also sustained his momentum through the vicissitudes of an uncertain world. As a child, he overcame not simply the loss of his mother but the dissolution of his family. He put in time in the trenches throughout his youth, earning his service stripes in the coal industry and studying on his own to make opportunities for advancement. Exercising the power available to a man of his day, he did so judiciously. While he made a way for himself, he enabled others to make their way, too. Working to get ahead, he also contributed significantly to improve his community. Having never enjoyed a closeness with his siblings and parents, he showered affection on his wife and children, even as he held high expectations for them. A demanding but compassionate father, he always enjoyed the love and respect of his children. And the dynamo that he set up in each of them continued to fuel them throughout their lives. So powerful was his influence on us all that he was a felt presence in our household long after he had departed it.

Many people came to observe the passing of my grandfather, one of our town's most powerful dignitaries; the church was filled, not only with members of our congregation, but also with neighbors, townsfolk, and visitors from out of town. After the service, a procession of black Cadillacs and Chryslers led us from the church, out of town, onto the highway, and five miles east to Churchill Cemetery at McClellandtown. We buried Pop in the large Wright family plot that he had purchased decades earlier when the first of his infant children had died.

Following the services, a large gathering of family and friends at 201 shared a buffet and stories, laughing about Pop's adventures as a young man or noting a lesson from his proud conduct through the depression. Relatives from Up East were milling about. Captain Harrison and his wife and daughter, who had driven up for the funeral and who stayed at our house overnight, were renewing acquaintances and being introduced to folks they hadn't met. With all of the adults occupied, Pete and I sneaked into Pop's room. A collector of all sorts of gadgets and gizmos, he had drawers full of neat stuff. One contained his barbering tools, which he had used on us for many years until he became too ill to cut our hair. Other drawers held blue medicine bottles, Zippo lighters, flashlights, keys galore, all sorts of coins, political memorabilia, and marbles of all sizes and varieties. One drawer was locked, but Pete knew where to find the key. That's when I was surprised to learn some more news about Dad.

14

"MASONTOWN OFFICER KILLED IN GERMANY"

Masontown, Pennsylvania
December 1954

In Pop's drawer I found a yellowed newspaper clipping. The five-inch-high picture showed my dad in his formal dress uniform. The headline read, "Masontown Officer Killed in Germany." I leaned on the freshly made bed and started to read the article out loud.

"Read it to yourself. I already read it." Pete fingered the pearl sides of a penknife.

First Lieutenant Ewing R. McClelland, one of Masontown's best known men, was killed in action in Germany,
December 23, the War Department has notified his
widow, Mrs. Marianna Wright McClelland, teacher in the
Masontown borough schools.

Leaving for overseas in October, 1944, the 28-year-old
officer had seen action in France, Belgium, and Germany.
He was with the 589th Field Artillery Battalion, 106th
Division. Enlisting before Pearl Harbor, he was commis-
sioned second lieutenant and trained in Camp Lee, Va.,
Camp Pickett, Va., Fort Sill, Okla., and Fort Bragg, N.C.

Lt. McClelland was a graduate of Masontown High
school, where he starred on the gridiron, and later
attended the University of Southern California. He was
a member of the First Presbyterian Church of Masontown and also a member of the Valley Lodge, No. 459,
Free and Accepted Masons.

In addition to his widow, he is survived by three
children, Ewing, Benjamin, and Mary Jane; his parents,
Mr. and Mrs. Ewing McClelland, of Masontown; one
sister, Mrs. Anna Dailey, wife of Ted Dailey, former Pitt
star, of Coatesville; two brothers, Sgt. James in France,
and Lester, at home.

Two brothers-in-law serve overseas, First Lieutenant
Ben F. Wright with the paratroopers in Belgium, and
First Lieutenant Thomas H. Wright with the Ordnance
Division in France. They are the sons of Mr. and Mrs.
R. K. Wright, of Masontown.

Such information about Dad was a rare find. Even though some things were incorrect, such as dad's age and the university he attended, certain details made indelible impressions on me.

"*[H]e starred on the gridiron . . .*" I knew that Uncle Les, the youngest in my dad's family, was also an All-American high school tackle. In college he starred at Syracuse University and had a brief pro career before distinguishing himself in the air force, eventually as a long-time captain of *Air Force One*. Les always credited football for launching him out of little Masontown into a world of opportunities. But I had never thought that my dad was a star athlete, too. No wonder people thought Pete and I would be good at sports. We never lived up to the expectations. What would growing up with a jock dad have done for our game?

"*[T]he 28-year-old-officer . . .*" The age stuck with me, even though, for the longest time, I couldn't really figure out what being twenty-eight was like. But the closer I got to that age myself, the more palpable became my vision of my dad as a vigorous young man. When I turned twenty-eight, it felt momentous. I thought, "So, it was now. This is as long as he lived. Now I feel some of the same things he did." As I sustained this vicarious sensation, my recurring thought was, "I wouldn't want to die now. I haven't achieved enough, seen enough, felt enough—lived enough." Believing that my dad must have had the same thought made me miserably sad. For a time I took some solace in A. E. Housman's sentiments on the wisdom of an athlete dying young:

> *Smart lad, to slip betimes away*
> *From fields where glory does not stay,*
> *And early though the laurel grows*
> *It withers quicker than the rose.*
>
> . . . .
>
> *Now you will not swell the rout*
> *Of lads that wore their honours out,*
> *Runners whom renown outran*
> *And the name died before the man.*

However, my dad had walked away from his glory days at least six years before his death. He had left his studies and his plans for a career in optometry, returned home, eloped with my mom, and joined the army. As the years passed, I began thinking more about his loss, not just mine. The family milestones he never attended. The current events he never witnessed. The daily comforts of living to a ripe age he never enjoyed. He missed the joyous victory-day celebrations. He missed the arrival of the huge TV console with the small screen that broadcast black-and-white pictures. He never got to enjoy the educational benefits of the GI bill. He never cheered as his younger brother Les played football, nor marveled as he piloted *Air Force One*. Years later, when my brother and I compared notes, these missed opportunities were what bothered him most, too, about Dad's early death.

Like the news clipping, other reminders popped up without warning. Once when Uncle Lloyd was showing us 8mm home movies of family vacations and Christmases, he put on an old reel. Watching the flickering white light projected on a sheet tacked to the living room wall, I saw a handsome, lanky man with dark hair, strolling back and forth in front of our house, holding two chubby-faced babies in beautiful knit outfits, so white against his army uniform. He smiled proudly into the camera. I wished so hard for my own real-life memories of him. But none would come. Ever.

Two years older, Pete did have some recollections about Dad. He reported seeing Mom the night she learned of Dad's death. He said that no adults believed him when he later related it:

> "You were too young to remember anything," they said. I was just under three years old. Mae Blaney came to stay with Mom after she learned Dad was killed. Mom's bedroom door was kept closed. I was pestering Mae to let me in. "I want to see my mommy." She took me over to the bed and Mom was lying face down, sobbing in her pillows. I patted her back but I'm sure she did not even know anyone was there.
>
> Another memory: Mom was standing at her chest of drawers holding Dad's picture and dabbing tears from her eyes. I asked, "When is my dad getting home?" She screamed at me, "Your dad's a war hero and he's never coming home!" Mom was crying and I was hugging her leg and crying.

Another time he recalled being with Mom when she was cleaning her closet:

> Mom was cleaning out her closet. I was real young and nebbing into everything. There was a suit box labeled "Pete's Robes." I was old enough to read it and was curious. Mom said, "Those are your dad's robes. You can have them when you get older." I opened the box and I think I had a flashback memory when I saw the wine-

> colored robe. Dad was wearing the wine robe holding
> me while Mom was squeezing oranges in a strange
> kitchen. Must have been at a camp in Virginia. I had to
> be less than two years old and the texture and color of
> the robe triggered the recall. (Amy has the robes, still
> in the same box.)

Although I wasn't conscious of it for a long time, my perception of my dad was changing over the years—and, of course, would continue to do so. For example, what had begun as so private a view of him as just my dad, a man in my family, evolved into a growing awareness of him as a man with a public history as well. The townspeople at the Memorial Day program, visitors to the war memorial at the schoolyard, area newspapers' readers, football fans, fellow miners—many people knew him, indeed, knew him well before I did.

In time, we children would hear snippets about our dad and mom. In their childhood years, for example, as they were growing up in the same church, singing in the same choir, and eventually singing duets, with Dad's sister, Anna, playing accompaniment, they became friends and then sweethearts. In high school, when he created such a flurry of excitement as a football star, Mom was always there as an admirer, although not a wholly uncritical one. Apparently, he rode the tide of public favor for all it was worth, including dating around a good bit. Then, he traveled to California to begin college. But after a year away, he returned home and began working in the mine with his father. When Mrs. Wells made the match between him and Mom, he soon decided she was the one with whom he would build his future as a family man.

In casual conversation over the years, my mom occasionally mentioned things about her life with Dad. If we seemed to put him on a pedestal, she would show us his clay feet, saying, for example, that he was basically a high school football star who still heard the roar of the crowd in his ears. He had enjoyed press clippings and a large popular following, including the adulation of local girls. When we mentioned his and Watty Tassone's feat of digging and loading in a single day the record amount of forty tons of coal, Mom said that she remembered it, adding wryly, "He wasn't much good that night."

Mom seemed to hold some pride in the fact that after years of being a ladies' man, he picked her when he looked for a serious love interest. At some point, she must have learned of the extent of his dating life before they married, because among the things Mom left behind, my sister found a booklet with girls' names and phone numbers, and my brother found a leather notebook binder from Dad's college days on the inside covers of which he had written several more girls' names and phone numbers, both from the campus and from his hometown area. Nevertheless, she stated with satisfaction that Dad left college, "came home and married me."

Mom also recalled her worry over my dad's favorite pastime: playing poker. When he was still in high school, my dad, Mack Wells, and other school buddies learned to play tennis, to wing shoot, and to play cards from Mack's dad, Doc Wells. Late into many summer nights, seated at a table on his screened-in back porch, Doc dealt blackjack, five-card stud, and draw poker to Masontown's youthful elite. As it turned out, my dad developed a keen intelligence for the game. Nobody would ever call him a card sharp, Mom said, but he remembered every card turned up during a blackjack game and could estimate with great accuracy the odds of a poker hand winning when the smoke grew thick and the pot grew large. When he was out of school and working in the mine, Dad became a regular in poker games in town. According to Mom, he kept a bank account in Carmichaels, a town across the river near the mine, because he didn't want local folks knowing how his luck was running.

One morning, after a long night of card playing, Dad awoke late and drove to Bessimer, where his father's crew was working in a slope mine, the shaft of which began on a hillside and dropped for a couple of miles down a gradual incline to the coal seam. At the beginning and end of the shift, the crew rode in and out on a mule-drawn coal wagon. Arriving late, Dad had to walk into the work area, guided only by the weak, yellow light of his cap lantern. When he met up with the crew, after about a twenty-minute hike, Dad approached the boss (his father), and said, "I'm here."

"We don't need you today," the boss replied flatly, looking with steely blue eyes at Dad, who was left to make his way back out of the slope and to contemplate a day's lost wages.

Because Dad and Mom eloped just before he enlisted, they spent some time apart, until he was stationed at Camp Lee, Virginia. He was close enough to return home on weekends when he could find a ride or could afford the bus. After a while, he found a room near the camp where she could come to stay on weekends. Eventually, they got an apartment in army housing. She and my brother also joined him for some time at Camp Pickett, Virginia. Amidst her recollections of all the fun they had socializing with new people, going out to dinner and to the movies, or dancing at the Officers' Club, she had less happy memories of Dad's card playing. She said that she rued the day that Doc Wells dealt the first hand. As a regular player on the base, Dad had both good and bad runs of luck. During the droughts, rather than dressing for dinner and an evening at the club, Mom had to heat a can of soup for them to share. After having to scrape by once too often between pay periods, Mom put her fist down, according to her. They argued and then reached a compromise. Dad was allotted a set sum from each paycheck for gambling. Mom had charge of the rest. This way she enjoyed the luxuries that my dad's winning brought without suffering poverty when Lady Luck failed to smile on him.

That wasn't, however, the end to their disagreements over his diversion. One night when they had returned to Masontown for a time, he went out to play with some hometown buddies. Tired of waiting alone for him to come home, Mom drove uptown to the Fort Mason Hotel, where he was playing, and laid on the car's horn until he came out and went home with her. He was amused and laughed about her antics, but she was angry, she reported.

In telling these anecdotes, Mom would laugh, but she also intended them as moral lessons for my brother and me, whom she secretly feared would develop our dad's penchant for playing cards. As it turned out, she should have fretted over my sister, who became the queen of the teenage hearts players. Once, when Mom walked past the dining room door and heard Mary Jane shuffling the cards, she stopped and remarked, "I've heard the deck riffled like that before!"

We twins were grown when Mom laughingly told us Dad's side of the night of our birth. Dad had been granted leave and so was able to go to the hospital with Mom. Warren Lesley, a family friend who was a year or so younger than Dad, was interning in pediatrics and attended our births. After Dad had spent some time pacing in the waiting room, Warren opened the door and reported, "Pete, you've got a baby boy. I have to go back. I think there's more to come." Not long afterwards, he returned again, reporting, "Pete, you have a baby girl, too." When Warren turned to leave, Dad said,

"Hey, you SOB! Don't you go in and get me any more children. Two is plenty."

Other than these incidents, Mom rarely spoke about our dad. My sister asked me recently if I thought Mom was courageous in holding it all inside—her lifelong love and the grief she felt over losing him—or if she was cowardly in hiding from it. I responded that I thought there was a little of both in her. A proud and privileged woman who had grown up in a man's world, Mom carried herself with a stoical demeanor in public. Still, as a highly sensitive woman with a vulnerable inner self, she tried to avoid facing the loss and loneliness that must have haunted her and might well have made her dysfunctional if she had let them. Living independently, as her brothers did, Mom successfully carried out her work as postmaster. I recall the stress and tension when male postal inspectors came periodically to examine her operation.

"They try to trip you up. You know, find some little thing on the books to rattle you. And they're always changing regulations, so you have to keep up with things. I won't let them get my goat," she'd say, showing as much pluck as anyone, male or female, could muster. Of course, her experienced assistant and first cousin Bruce Sterling partnered decisions with her, the two of them having a good working relationship throughout the years.

And so it was that she lived, raising three children (with help from her mother and nannies, to be sure), carrying on her business career, socializing with family and with women friends, and rejecting suitors' proposals. It seems to me that she must have been particularly courageous to remain independent in the years just following the war. In her late twenties, she turned down two childhood sweethearts, each of whom, in turn, came back to pledge his love for her and to ask for her hand in marriage. Through it all, she sustained a single-minded dedication to Dad. She undoubtedly took to eating as a compensatory activity. She also watched musicals time and again, just as she lost herself reading love stories. And every day, she'd read her horoscope, as if it might somehow bring her a happy fate. I didn't know whether she really believed that eating pork roast and sauerkraut on New Year's Day would bring good luck all year, or if she did it for the sheer gustatory delight. Maybe both.

And then, there were her surrogate children, the poodles she cared for in her twenty-two-year retirement period. To fill up her empty nest we got her a toy poodle pup for a companion. Mom named her Gigi, after the character in one of her favorite musicals. Of course, our uncles helped us to pay the three-hundred-dollar cost. Gigi was a silver poodle, but as a pup, she was still black-haired. When Uncle Lloyd first saw her, he said, "I thought she was supposed to be silver."

"Oh, she'll turn silver as she grows older," I said.

Picking her up, he said jokingly to Gigi, "You better turn to silver, by God."

Mom raised and eventually bred Gigi, yielding a litter of two males and two females. Although she was supposed to part with these pups, Mom couldn't bear to and, therefore, raised all of them. After about thirteen years, Gigi died. Misty, the outgoing female pup, became the top dog. After the pups reached a ripe old age, they, too, died, one after another. Mom soon got a new pup, Peaches, her companion till Mom's last months. On rare occasions we boarded Peaches at a kennel, so that Mom could travel with us. Mom enjoyed the trips, but nothing was sweeter to her than the homecoming reunion with Peaches.

Of Mom's ability to carry it all off on her own, I have to acknowledge that such unusual strength of character—such stubborn persistence to be her own person, in the face of great odds—is remarkable, but understandable for a woman who came from the stock of Deborah Lloyd and R. K. Wright.

15

FIRST LOVE

Masontown, Pennsylvania
1958–1961

I found myself in the middle of a difficult adolescence. Is there any other kind? Like all teenagers, I assume, I felt so different from the adults in my family. Having been a teacher's pet and having identified with adult authority, this sense of estrangement was new and uncomfortable. I looked more to Pete and Mary Jane— although we had developed into such different individuals with separate sets of friends and interests. My classmate Ronnie Smith and I took late-night drives and philosophized, as well as we could, about what we were experiencing. The entertainment world exploded with diversions that became our main attractions. Our parents hated rock 'n' roll, this strange, loud music, and the gyrating scene it ushered in. So much the better, we thought. Piles of 45s littered our living room floor around the stereo. We boys drove to rural hideaways, puffed cigarettes, and swigged beer. We tried new clothes and hairstyles in an effort to look less like kids but not as old as the grown-ups.

I was in the middle of this youth culture and yet not wholly of it. There was a part of me that just wanted to put the teen years behind me and be an adult. I felt headed somewhere. I was driven to succeed. Undeniably, it was an ego thing. Since I was only modestly talented, I worked hard to achieve what came easily to the class geniuses. I acted in school plays and reveled in the attention. I was president of the student government and took the leadership role very seriously, sometimes for the wrong reasons. Rightly or wrongly, I attributed some of this drive, this attempt to be top dog, to being a middle child. I also ascribed some of it to growing up in the shadow of a war hero father. Even though I never expected to match his sacrifice, I wanted to be a good man, like he was. I wanted to prove something to him.

And I wanted everyone who admired him to admire me, too. This yearning, this unnamed pressure, this sense of expectations evolved.

At twelve, I learned firsthand about the birds and the bees, thanks to a friendly older girl. When I began dating, I fell hard in love, going with just one girl at a time, very seriously, very faithfully, and very melodramatically. And then I met Anita.

In eighth grade, she sang "He" onstage at All Saints, the Catholic school. Seeing the spotlight on her—she wore a pale purple, satin dress—and listening to the bell-like clarity of her soprano voice, I was transported by her beauty, the sight and the sound. She sang with such heartfelt dedication, such love, such commitment. However ephemeral it may have been, I felt as devoted to her at that moment as she was to Him.

A petite Mediterranean beauty with shiny, dark hair and bright brown eyes, Anita was intelligent, highly motivated, and quick to smile. Her laugh was wonderfully musical. A majorette who was very popular, she had pep and bounce in her step as she worked through her march-and-twirling routines. Always neat in appearance, she carried herself with feminine grace and aplomb. If anything at all could be found amiss, it was perhaps that her self-esteem may have been a bit low, because she was the youngest of three girls whose mother played favorites.

How to reveal the truth of this puppy love that grew into a powerful, long-term first love? We found each other as soul mates in the first decade of rock 'n' roll. Elvis's "Love Me Tender" and dozens of other songs of teenage love defined the many moments of desire and frustration that characterized our relationship. Anita was a fully passionate young woman who always acted morally in step with her sound Roman Catholic faith, even though I would continually challenge her with sexual desire in the moonlight on sultry summer nights and on frosty winter eves. She wanted to be good to me and true to herself. Given my wanton desire, she must have been conflicted. Looking back on it now, I see myself as an unscrupulous and hypocritical teenage boy, wanting physical love without deserving it through personal commitment to a lasting relationship.

Even if I pledged eternal, undying love along with the lyrics of the songs, I didn't really know what I was saying, couldn't really have meant it, except as a fervent, hormone-driven fantasy. I wanted to live in the moment. I wanted to consummate that desire. The palpable fear of the bomb extinguishing us at any moment seemed my ally in this cause.

Yet, in addition to our physical attraction, Anita and I really cared for each other, liked each other as friends, had fun together, talked and talked and talked to each other about our families, about the current events of the day, and about the ideals by which we hoped to live.

We often discussed our differing religious traditions. We were committed to our respective faiths, but the immediacy of our bonding was so strong that we abided with each other's beliefs, not needing to attempt changing either person's convictions. We believed that we could negotiate a mixed marriage to our mutual satisfaction. In each of our families were examples of such couples. Only once do I recall us both being made uncomfortable in her home: after being introduced to me and shaking my hand, a large, forty-something priest turned to Anita's mother and asked, "Is he Catholic?"

"No," she replied, trying her best to maintain a smile.

"Take him out back and drown him in the creek." The priest attempted or feigned a joke, but said it in such an unpleasant tone that the slight titter that arose in the room quickly died away. He never looked at me again during his visit, until he nodded his head in my direction on his way out the door.

Truth be told, I was always heavy maintenance, as lovers went. I was highly attentive, giving cards, observing birthdays and anniversaries, showering affection, wanting to touch, eager to express feelings. All of this intensely—to a fault. To a fault, because I expected the same kind and level of interaction in return. I had heard of unselfish, undemanding love, but I didn't practice it. Because I made few close friends, and because I related better to women than to men, I made the relationship with my sweetheart bear more freight than was reasonable to expect. Anita bore this well; she was a caring, nurturing companion.

Anita's note to me on the inside cover of Harper Lee's *To Kill a Mockingbird*, a present to me in 1960, showed her deep passion for life and her kindheartedness:

> To Benny,
> As a remembrance never to kill mockingbirds and of the many times we've talked of this with happiness.
> With much love & affection
> Anita Louise
> P.S. This is the most precious thing I could give to you.

There were brief moments of apostasy in my love, I must admit. Summers meant three weeks away at Boy Scout and church camps. In my case, absence from my true love made my heart grow fonder for someone nearby. A week at church camp was just long enough to launch a superficial flirtation. No doubt the girl also had a boyfriend back home, but since we lived a couple of hundred miles apart, we knew the fling wouldn't last much longer than a letter or two after we left camp. The summer between my junior and senior years, a sweet girl and I had an especially intense physical relationship, often sneaking off to a wooded worship circle aptly christened "God's Little Acre." Our devotion was entirely secular; we profaned the sacred spot. Our only punishment? A worldly one. Mosquito bites in abundance. In the panting, heady rush of our naked play, we never noticed the bloodlust of hundreds of mosquitoes who enjoyed our outings as much as we did. Months later in the fall, Anita found an after-camp love letter that I had negligently discarded in the car's glove compartment. She was deeply, tearfully hurt, as she deserved to be. I was guilty as charged, but the passion of the summertime fancy was long gone, just a fond memory in my male mind. After a long night of accusation and explanation, of recommitment and forgiveness, we made up. What my infidelity may have done to Anita's trust in me, I'll never know. She was too gracious to ever bring it up again.

Anita's parents treated me wonderfully. Her mother was ever gracious, always invited me to the table with them, and thoughtfully asked after my family. Her dad was a special person who meant a great deal to me and who treated me grandly. His life followed an upward trajectory, as did Pop's, but as an Italian immigrant, Guiseppe DeRosa had to overcome more obstacles. With a great deal of pluck, he made a good life for himself and his family. When I was a youngster, he ran Prince's Inn, a popular restaurant and bar between Masontown and Smithfield where Uncle Tom and Aunt Rose and their friends regularly dined and danced. The restaurant's name came from the moniker by which Anita's dad was known. Prince was a strikingly handsome Sicilian, always dressed to kill as he hosted his guests. While less than six feet tall, he was barrel-chested and had large, cleanly defined muscles. Powerfully built as he was, Prince had settled a lot of scores in his rough-and-tumble world. Yet, Prince much preferred laughing to fighting; I should say roaring, because he had a hearty, raucous, whole-body laugh. Once he told me— very graphically—about punching a stubborn cow in the nose to get it to move. He laughed so hard that he could hardly describe the blood pouring out of the cow's nose and the pain in his aching hand. We both ended up hanging onto each other laughing till tears flowed. As I wiped my eyes and watched him gain his composure, I marveled at him and dearly appreciated feeling so close to a man outside my family.

Whenever we went to her family's get-togethers, I stuck close to Prince. I didn't know the others so well and I knew if I was near him, I'd hear some good stories. Of course, there were times when he didn't want me to stick by him. Once at a large, family picnic in an outdoor pavilion, I noticed Prince slowly walking a short distance from the crowd. I followed him, calling to him as I went. The closer I got, the more he retreated. We danced that way, moving like chess pieces, farther and farther from the pavilion. Finally, he broke wind, loudly and with an obvious sense of relief. As soon as he did, he also broke into a roaring laugh, as he said in his broken English, "'At's why I keep trying to get away from you."

When Anita and I were in high school, Prince closed the time-consuming restaurant business and ran a beverage distributorship out of the building on the second floor of which they lived. After Anita and I had dated for a year or so, Prince invited me downstairs and offered me a cold bottle of Iron City beer. It was an act of friendship, man to man, and I felt his sincerity as we talked together. Frequently, before Anita and I went out, he called me aside and pulled cash out of his pocket, asking me if I needed any. I never did, but his act of generosity was never lost on me.

What happened to end such a deep, meaningful relationship? During our senior year we wore each other like comfortable shoes. We were in love. Each of us celebrated with and suffered with the other. We were a part of each other's family, at home in either place. We had become as important to each other's well-being as our families were. We shared our last year's milestones together: the ceremonies at the new school building, the plays, the ball games, and the dances. However, late in the spring, after Anita decided to attend nursing school in Pittsburgh and I decided to attend college a hundred miles farther north in Grove City, the past and pres-

ent—which had been all-consuming in my consciousness—dissolved to nothing, as the future, the unknown
days ahead, loomed on my horizon. So, I forced a
breakup. My ego was pushing me to achieve something
bigger than whatever our little world held out for us, I
thought at the time. Undoubtedly more emotionally
committed to our partnership, Anita wanted us to continue our relationship after graduation. Only after my
repeated insistence did she remove my high school ring
and throw it across her living room floor in an unwill-
ing defeat, sobbing tearfully in grief at the loss.

I felt the loss deeply, too, but believed that breaking
free was something that I needed to do. Still, it hurt to
lose such a love. I had grown to be a different person
with her as my constant companion. Now, I suffered
vertigo. Who was I now that I was making a solo flight?
I would sing along repeatedly with Little Anthony and
the Imperials, letting the stereo replay "Tears on My Pil-
low" until someone in the house insisted on a change,
whereupon I'd search for another heartbroken lament.

Actually, although we dated others, Anita and I kept
in touch a good deal throughout our first year after high
school. I traveled to Pittsburgh for occasional dates and,
at home in the summer, we saw each other some,

though infrequently. Compared to our earlier easygoing, warm togetherness, these were polite, somewhat guarded meetings, especially on my part. With arrogance of ambition I had torn myself free of our love. So callous had I become to any rapprochement between us that one summer night, when she invited a recommitment to our erstwhile passionate relationship, I calculatingly refused to engage at that level. As long as I live, the irony of this moment will haunt me. After three years of striving to make love with this adorable woman, I refused her full offering of herself. With Anita, on the whole, I was a loving partner; however, in this act, I regret to say, I was basely self-protective.

I cannot underestimate the value of this first love, not just for what it offered me at the time, but also what it has meant over the years—because Anita was so considerate and generous long after we stopped seeing each other. When she returned home to visit her parents, she also continued to visit my mother, even though she knew that I was far away. She returned for high school class reunions—which I did not—and asked Mary Jane to give me her regards. After she quietly married, Anita wrote me a long, caring letter, explaining her special feeling for me: I was no longer her love, but would always remain her first love. At almost every crisis in my life, I have thought of Anita, wanted to call her, to counsel and confer with her. But, oddly reticent, I never did. Recently, in the composing of this book, we did speak by telephone again. Forty years after our time together—despite how far we have journeyed from those young lovers that we were—when we talked, long-distance, we each still felt a special bond with the other, our first love.

16

"SPEAK THE SPEECH, I PRAY THEE, TRIPPINGLY ON THY TONGUE"

Masontown, Pennsylvania
Fall 1960

Just before my senior year, 1960–1961, my hometown high school merged with several smaller ones and the one in Pt. Marion, a nearby rival town, to form a new school. The new building was located between the two towns at Friendship Hill on land donated by Albert Gallatin's estate. I was elected the first student government president and, therefore, was designated to deliver a speech in mid-April on behalf of the consolidated student body at the dedication of the new school building.

My speech at the dedication ceremony was a stirring success. Applause echoed off the shiny, hardwood floor in the new auditorium-gymnasium. Dr. Charles Bryan, a former principal at Pt. Marion's high school, delivered the main address, stating as one of his points that inspiration is a key to education. Departing from his notes, Bryan remarked that, indeed, in delivering my speech, I had been an example of such inspiration in education. Then, he paused and called me to the podium, leading the crowd in a standing ovation. The *Dominion-News*, from Morgantown, West Virginia, the nearest city, carried a front-page story and four pictures of the event. One picture showed me standing on the dais with Dr. Bryan and the school district superintendent. Tom Mills, the paper's city editor and the article's author, summarized much of Dr. Bryan's speech and editorialized on my appearance.

> One of the speakers on the program, not so much by what he said but the way in which he said it and the fact that he did say it, served as a "living example" of what Dr. Bryan said.

That speaker was the president of the Albert Gallatin student body, a tall, handsome, alert, and healthy looking boy named Ben McClelland. His appearance, his courage was indeed a high point in the program—an INSPIRA-TION—as it were to his fellow students, to the officials, and to the patrons and friends of the school.

Ben McClelland's brief, but pungent talk on behalf of the student body served to let the people know the students appreciated "our new school" built on land "steeped in the early tradition of the United States . . ."

"Albert Gallatin," he said, "would be pleased to know his land was now the site of an educational center named for him."

Albert Gallatin, fourth secretary of the Treasury of the United States under Presidents Jefferson and Madison, had given many of his years to bringing industries to the Point Marion area.

Receiving such public recognition was a heady trip: "Hometown boy makes good" and all that. In fact, I did get a swelled head. I recall leaving the ceremony with Anita, who was thoroughly disgusted with my swaggering through the departing crowd, as I received even more adulation. Unlike her, few people knew the story behind the story: how an inexperienced schoolboy made a remarkable public address. In fact, I owed my performance to two mentors, Marino Pierattini and my

namesake uncle. A lawyer and amateur historian, Uncle
Ben helped me write a detailed and upbeat speech that
recalled the school site's patriotic history during the
Revolutionary War years and the early days of the
republic. Uncle Ben knew a number of historical details,
including that Gallatin had built and operated a muni-
tion factory there, from which he sold war supplies to
the colonists. Because he was a former debater and
because, as a lawyer, Uncle Ben routinely dictated letters
and briefs into a tape machine for his secretary to type,
he had developed a keen skill for thinking through a
subject and dictating it in well-organized, perfectly cor-
rect, and stylish sentences. I memorized the text verba-
tim. Then, in several after-school sessions, my high
school English and speech teacher, Mr. Pierattini,
worked with me on my delivery to develop timing,
emphasis, and gestures—rhetorical techniques to carry
the message across a podium to a large audience. So, as
a novice public speaker who turned in such a high-level
performance, I actually owed my success to the tutelage
of two experts.

More than that, however, in this particular case the
three of us were playing out the denouement of an
American story that began in the first years of the

colonies and climaxed two decades before the speech. Uncle Ben and Perry—as we referred to Mr. Pierattini—were not only experts of history and of rhetoric, but they also shared a unique history. About two decades before my speech, my uncle had been Perry's student. In fact, it was under Perry's coaching that Uncle Ben and his team became the state debate champions. Then, in a harsh twist of fate shortly after my uncle's graduation from high school, these two men found themselves in very different circumstances: serving America in the Second World War. Just as Uncle Ben dropped out of college to enlist, Perry left his job and signed up. As a native speaker of Italian, Perry wound up in the Allied command structure in the European theater of war. In the midst of the difficult winter fighting in Italy, Uncle Ben was summoned to headquarters from his freezing foxhole on a mountainside. Captain Pierattini greeted him and, after coffee and small talk, gave him two large candles to use in the foxhole. It didn't stave off the frostbite that got to Uncle Ben's toes, but the gesture warmed their relationship for the rest of their lives.

So it was that two decades later, these two men extended their collaboration into the next generation, working with me on the dedication speech. Not only did the new school building represent an act of faith in the future, but also our speech at its dedication connected it to the founding spirit of our nation. In schools during the cold war years of the late fifties and early sixties, the old and the young, even with their dissimilar personal histories, were able to cooperate to carry on such American cultural traditions. Perry and Uncle Ben were motivated by their personal histories in the fight against totalitarianism. As a teacher, Perry devoted his life to helping young people, through the power of language and rhetoric, participate in a democratic society. As a lawyer, Uncle Ben served to help people enjoy the legal protections of a just society. When I spoke the speech as they helped me shape it, I adopted that prevailing ideology, as well.

At graduation exercises at the end of the school year, I was given the American Legion award for leadership. Guiding the student government over that first year and delivering that speech at the school dedication doubtless were the major factors in my receiving the award. I will forever be indebted to my mentors for enabling me to achieve such a distinction. As a way of showing them my gratitude, when I became a teacher and published a textbook three decades later, I dedicated it to three teachers: Edith Magliotti, my high school math and French teacher, Perry, and Patricia Ford, my college English teacher. Each had taught me that learning is a way of life.

However, less than a decade after that speech, civil and social unrest against oppression within our own society changed the way old and young, students and teachers, related to each other. Following in the best of the intellectual tradition that my mentors had exemplified, I felt called to strike out on a path very different from the one they had taken. Nurtured by them in a tradition of educational conservators—passing along unquestioningly the ethos of the American dream—I, however, teach according to a different pedagogy. I teach students to adopt a skeptical, interrogating, critical consciousness. Following an intellectual tradition that evolved out of the sixties' social revolution, I question the hegemonic structures that have prevailed, because that traditional approach failed, I contend, to provide its promises of freedom and equality to Americans of both sexes and of all races, colors, and creeds. Of course, I cannot show much surprise when I observe in my students little desire to interrogate current American ideology, but rather a strong interest in entering contemporary society on its terms.

It's painful for me to consider that—after the cataclysmic social forces of the sixties that changed American society forever—Uncle Ben, Perry, and I could no longer sustain the common bond and the unwavering belief in the simple ideal of American society that we did in that speech in 1960. During my lifetime, I was never called upon to make the sacrifices that they did in serving in World War II—not to mention my dad's ultimate sacrifice. Nevertheless, striving to follow their example, I can try to acquit myself with a measure of their principled character, their intellectual integrity, and their personal courage when facing the challenges my world asks of me.

17

IF YOU VALUE FREEDOM, SEEK JUSTICE

Masontown, Pennsylvania

It reads like any carefully composed, respectful letter of sympathy. But it was an unusual letter, written by a reticent young man who never mailed it to the surviving widow. Following Uncle Ben's death, his former law partner, John Hemington, wrote a letter of sympathy to Aunt Frankie. In this very long epistle, Mr. Hemington summed up the qualities of the man he knew so well and revered so much. For unexplained reasons, he never mailed the letter until after Aunt Frankie's death, when

he sent it to her and Uncle Ben's daughter, my cousin
Deb. I saw it when Deb, touched by Mr. Hemington's
deep respect for her father, passed it on to my sister.

> Anyone who knew Ben, knew what a fine person he was,
> but many probably never recognized what a wonderfully
> skilled attorney he was. Ben always gave the impression,
> I thought, of the wily old country lawyer who was not
> quite up to speed on the issue at hand, yet nothing could
> have been further from the truth. He loved the law, rel-
> ished it, studied it, understood the value of preparation,
> and never, ever, as far as I knew, did anything halfway....
> In addition to his other fine qualities, Ben was the most
> honest and compassionate individual I have ever
> known—in or out of the legal profession. It is an honor
> and a privilege to have known him....
>
> There is no person, aside from my parents, who has
> had a greater impact on my life and thought—no one I
> respected more than Ben Wright—he was a friend, a
> mentor, and a guiding light. There is no way I can ever
> live up to the standard he set, but I can certainly love and
> appreciate the Standard Bearer. Ben will live forever in
> the hearts of those who knew and loved him and, in the
> long run, that is all anyone can ask.

Born in 1920, Benjamin Franklin Wright, my namesake uncle, also had a namesake: Old Ben, his paternal

grandfather, who had been born Up East in Plymouth, Pennsylvania, in 1846. Uncle Ben, the baby of the family, was a jovial and bright youngster with energy to burn. Uncle Ben and his first cousin Ebenezer Lloyd Lewis grew up as best buddies. While stories about their youthful pursuits abound, one involves Tommy Dick as an unwitting informant. As a grade-schooler, Tommy Dick routinely came home for lunch and returned for the afternoon session. One day he loitered about until Grandma asked if it wasn't time for him to get back to school.

"Oh, I want to stick around and see what Ben and Eben are going to do."

"What do you mean?"

"Well, when I was coming home, I saw them jump out of one of the high school windows. So, I thought I would wait to see if they came here."

With that knowledge, Grandma told Tommy Dick to hightail it back to school that minute. She hurried through the alley to her sister's house where they found the two truants, happily occupying themselves in the garage. The sisters escorted their two rascals back to school and had a good laugh about it on the way home.

In high school, Uncle Ben excelled in literature and languages, and he acquitted himself honorably in public speaking, becoming captain of the debate team, and—showing that the Wright pedigree extended all the way down to him—he carried his debate team to victory in the state championship. Following his oldest brother's path to college at nearby Waynesburg, he would soon make his own way in life.

On that fateful Sunday—December 7, 1941—when the Japanese attacked Pearl Harbor, Uncle Ben and Eben decided to enlist in the army together. Thinking that they could serve in the army side by side, just as they had lived their lives in Masontown, Eben and Uncle Ben drove that Sunday afternoon to the army recruiter's office in Uniontown, which was open, despite it being Sunday, because of the aggression on our Hawaiian Islands. At daybreak the next morning, so the family story goes, when Uncle Lloyd and Aunt Sally were leaving their home in Waynesburg for work, Uncle Ben was sitting on the curb with all of his belongings packed, waiting to hitch a ride with them to Masontown. Unfortunately for them, Uncle Ben and Eben were separated shortly after they enlisted, when interest and aptitude tests pointed them in different directions.

Thus, leaving college midway through his freshman year, he volunteered as a private in the army. After completing Officers' Candidate School in field artillery, he scrapped his way (at five feet, eight inches) into the 101st Airborne Division and fought in all of the major campaigns in the European theater. He parachuted into the fray in North Africa and, later, Sicily. During the freezing winter campaign in Italy, he suffered such severely frostbitten feet that he was carried from his foxhole and trucked to a field hospital. The surgeons scheduled him for a double amputation, but cancelled it when his feet responded to physical therapy. (He suffered foot ailments the rest of his life and could never stand out in the cold.)

Rejoining his unit, he jumped onto the continent behind German lines on D-Day minus one. He held out in the muddy siege of Bastogne during the Battle of the Bulge, serving as a forward observer for the artillery. Suffering extreme hardships and facing untold dangers, he was awarded a Purple Heart and Bronze Star, among other awards, though he never displayed them. After four years of fierce combat, he returned home. Of those in his unit with whom he had gone overseas, only 20 percent survived the war.

Uncle Ben rarely talked about his war experiences, though he said that the world of the army at war was the forge that tempered him, transforming him from a boy into a man. My brother, who traveled frequently to Europe, once elicited a rare comment about the war from Uncle Ben. Pete told Uncle Ben about his trip to Margraten, The Netherlands, and his visit to Dad's grave in the American Military Cemetery. Uncle Ben asked Pete what nearby Aachen, Germany, looked like. When Pete said that it looked like a modern city, Uncle Ben retorted, "It should be modern. All we left standing were the cathedrals!"

Among his wartime notes, found posthumously, was an anecdote Uncle Ben had written in Nice, after the liberation of France, in which he revealed the difficulty he had exercising his humanitarian sensibilities in the complex moral climate in which he was implicated:

> The French had about 100 German prisoners there digging out the mines.
>
> Once a German P. W. got hit from a bouncing Betty mine and the French Medical Officer just looked at him like he was a dog. He then sent for one of the two enormously fat French nurses who wore dirty uniforms.
>
> I told the P. W.s to put the litter, which was a door from one of the houses, on the back of the jeep and I took off for the U.S. aid station. I was the hero of the

prisoners, but the Frenchmen were mad as hell. The report went up through French channels, then down through U.S. channels till my Bn. Commander, John T. Cooper, Jr., came to see me. I told him the whole story and then let him see their aid station and the dirty nurses. John just laughed and said, "Hell Brother Ben, you never could speak French worth a damn. How in the hell could you have known what those Frenchmen wanted you to do!"

The German P. W.s would smile when they saw me and would pet my dog, Banco, every chance they could. They were guarded by Gouma troops from North Africa who were quite cruel with the prisoners but when those same Germans were in charge, they invented new cruelty techniques.

So who was right—it was no place for a country boy who always looked at things like a cowboy movie. The good guys wore white hats. They had friends who were funny.

Back stateside after the war, Uncle Ben supplemented his GI bill benefits, working his way through college and law school as a journeyman carpenter. He married Doc Wells's daughter, Frances, and they moved to Washington, D.C., where Uncle Ben did a stint with the FBI. In 1952, we visited them, touring around all of the monuments. Uncle Ben gamely marched us up the stairs of the Washington Monument all the way to the top and then down again. When we reached the bottom, he turned around and—feigning—said, "Ready to head back up?" When we cheerily said, "Yes," he admitted that he was just kidding. Telling the story years later, he fessed up even more: his legs had gone numb. He and Aunt Frankie also took us to see historic Williamsburg, Virginia, where he gave us a running commentary filled with all sorts of interesting historical facts.

Returning to Masontown a few years later, Uncle Ben earned a law degree and built a well-respected law practice in neighboring Uniontown. He and Aunt Frankie raised a daughter, Debra Kathryn. Sharing her father's love for the truth and having inherited his public-speaking ability, D. K. Wright became a television news reporter and anchorwoman. (Using her initials, Deb made a connection to her grandfather, R. K. Wright, a subtlety that may have been lost on the rest of the world, but made her dad beam with pride.) In their tiny bungalow atop a hill next to Neff's Woods at the north end of town, Uncle Ben and Aunt Frankie gardened and raised a passel of cats and dogs. Besides their purebred dogs, a springer spaniel and a basset hound, there was a succession of mixed-breed critters that wandered by

and stayed for a lifetime, finding the animal-loving pro-
prietors and the accommodations to their liking.

Uncle Ben was a loving, attentive uncle who entertained us with tall tales. I remember his jolly chatter as
he supervised us in building a crude cabin in Neff's
Woods one summer. He also built us a playhouse. Not
just a simple design, this one featured a shuttered window that locked from the inside, a countertop across the
entire front (for lemonade sales!), a trapdoor in the
floor, and a ladder that led onto the roof. This latter feature was quite a bone of contention, with Mom objecting out of fear that we would break something if we fell
or jumped off the roof. Undeterred, Uncle Ben nailed
the ladder up, with Mom still loudly protesting. Even
though we were made to promise not to, we jumped off
the roof innumerable times. We suffered a few sprains
but no broken bones.

One summer, Uncle Ben also took us to the Gettys-
burg battlefield, recounting detail after detail of battle
strategy, as we tried to take in the sheer expanse of the
scene. Of course, as I saw the various soldiers' uniforms
and heard the muskets explode on the battlefield orien-
tation film, I thought ruefully about Dad. However, I

was also able to put his sacrifice into a context for the first time, as I came to understand that throughout the history of our nation, dads have been dying to preserve their life principles for their families.

I have returned to those sites of national treasure time and again over the years. Each time that I took my own children, I hoped that they would experience the same sense of awe that I did at seeing—and feeling— the history of our country. Whenever I come upon the black-and-white snapshots of our trips with Uncle Ben, I marvel at how simple and small we look. At the time, everything seemed so grand to me, so crammed full was I with historical information and brimming over with national pride.

Following his considerable experiences with air-planes during the war, Uncle Ben continued a keen interest in them. When airmail service came to town, he drove us up to Martin's Farm, the highest spot in the region, to see the mail pickup. What a marvel to see the plane fly slowly along, hook the heavy leather satchel, and roar away.

When we were youngsters, our uncles—especially Uncle Ben—participated actively in setting up our

Christmas celebrations. It's an understatement to say that folks went overboard, lavishing gifts on us, in order to ensure that we had a very merry Christmas. Even though the return of the holiday season brought Mom an annual reminder of her loss—Pete recalls many Christmases when he saw Mom face down on her bed, "sobbing her heart out"—she always made Christmas very special for us.

I remember being awakened one Christmas Eve by the adults talking and laughing in the living room. Walking into the room, I was rubbing my eyes, trying to see what all the commotion was about. Before I could get much of a glimpse, Uncle Ben scooped me up and carried me off to bed, telling me to stay put so Santa could come. Years later, when Pete and I got a tree at Preach Smith's store and tried to put it up ourselves for the first time, we botched the job. Because we had bought a tree that was too tall for our nine-foot ceiling, Pete and I sawed off a piece of the trunk and some lower branches in order to make it fit. After we put it in the base and set it upright, it fit perfectly; however, it was bare from the floor to about three feet up. Mom called on Uncle Ben to bail us out. Fetching a hammer and some tacks, Uncle Ben reconstructed the lower part of the tree, all the while chuckling, cracking jokes, and singing "Only God Can Make a Tree." The needles stayed green and on the boughs just long enough to save our holiday.

Whenever it snowed, we headed to his and Aunt Frankie's house on the tall knob at the end of town. He took us sled riding on his long, sloping hillside, ferrying us—after every run—back to the top in his Jeep. After we'd had enough, we piled into the kitchen where Aunt Frankie warmed us with hot cocoa, cookies, and her hospitality.

A collector of pistols and a champion marksman, Uncle Ben turned a small room in his basement into a gun workshop and display area filled with handguns in fine, green-felt-lined cases. A German Luger, a war souvenir, was among his prized possessions. When he thought I was old enough to handle a gun, he took me with him and his cousin Eben pistol shooting. Besides learning this new skill, I enjoyed the camaraderie of these close friends. They would tell jokes and, on rare occasion, talk about the war. Once when we were loading up our pistols, Eben remembered a story about his unit liberating one of the German concentration camps.

Eben and his buddy were ordered to go to the dog kennels and destroy the guard dogs. As they approached the kennels, they saw a group of healthy German shepherds with sleek coats. Some dogs sat quietly, some were lying down, and all turned their heads to watch the men approach. The buddy said, "Damn, Eben! Have you ever seen such beautiful animals in your entire life? I want to pick out a young one to keep." With that, he stepped up to the wire door and reached for the latch. In a flash several dogs bounded toward him, the closest two snapping at his hand through the wire. "You SOBs!" he screamed, jerking his hand back. (At this point in recounting the story to Uncle Ben and me, Eben acted out the part of his buddy, tucking one hand under his arm and pretending to shoot a pistol with his other hand.) "Blam! Blam! Blam! Blam! Blam! Blam! Blam!" After emptying his gun, the soldier reloaded and, still swearing under his breath, shot all of the dogs.

Different as they were, Uncle Ben and Eben shared more than pistol-shooting throughout their lifelong friendship. With Uncle Ben's avocation in carpentry and Eben's mechanical genius, they spent long evenings working on various projects. When Uncle Ben acquired a large, two-story, frame building that had once served as a chicken coop, they renovated it, including reroofing it, installing a new furnace, replacing rotten floorboards in the second floor, and repainting it. Outfitting it with a full complement of tools, the two whiled away many nights of their later years, trading stories and enjoying each other's company—and that of a few select friends, who were lucky enough to be welcome guests at the "Chicken Palace."

As secretary of the local bar association, Uncle Ben titillated his fellow members with his great sense of humor. Through a forty-year practice, he earned the reputation of being a formidable barrister and a man of unimpeachable integrity. He not only did pro bono work for the county but also regularly tried underdog cases for people who couldn't pay him.

Uncle Ben's last years demanded much personal sacrifice. Overweight and suffering from heart disease, he nonetheless continued practicing law. Aunt Frankie had had two battles with cancer. A woman with an iron will, she survived, but incurred exorbitant medical bills. Uncle Ben worked longer than someone in his poor health should have before he was finally able to retire. Unlike Mom's, his respite after a long career was short-lived.

We pushed Mom to Uncle Ben's funeral in a wheel-chair. Mom hated the funereal atmosphere and avoided "paying last respects" whenever possible. I remember Grandma saying to her once, "What if nobody goes to your funeral?"

"Good. I hope they don't. I don't want anybody look-ing at me laid out." Nevertheless, Mom bravely attended Uncle Ben's funeral. When her cousin and longtime coworker Bruce Sterling walked in, she smiled and said to him, "We're still here." Though failing, at eighty she was, indeed, still a survivor.

Back at 201 afterwards, we had a family dinner at the dining table that had served the Wright family for the better part of a century. Mom and Aunt Frankie were the only two of their generation in the family still living. The rest of us were the children or grandchildren of those in their generation. The dinner began as a somber affair, despite the abundance of favorite recipes in the old family dishes. Then, thinking about Uncle Ben at Grandma's funeral, I remembered how surprised I was to find him telling humorous family stories and making jokes. What he was doing, I realized, was trying to help people cope with their grief, to heal through laughter. So, when I found the opportunity, I inserted a one-liner into the conversation. And then another. Then I told an old family story. Others put in a line here and there. Before long, the room had warmed with laughter and stories, and we enjoyed a long mealtime.

When she was leaving, Aunt Frankie, tired and frail, paused in the hallway and thanked me for livening things up. "You know," she reminded me, "that's what your Uncle Ben did so well at these occasions."

"I know," I replied and gave her a good-bye hug.

It was our last family gathering at 201. The building was sold shortly thereafter. After existing for the better part of a century the Wright family home at 201 North Main Street was no longer.

18

GRANDMA WRIGHT

Bloomington, Indiana
March 16, 1966

Mom called and told me that Grandma had died after being hospitalized for four days.

"Four days! Why didn't you tell me?" I shouted.

"Grandma said not to. She didn't want you to worry. Listen, Ben, when we first admitted her, it was just for a foot infection. They found a needle in her heel; it had broken off below the eye. The doctor said he thought it had been there for a long time and something just irritated it recently."

"Well, what did she die of?"

"A stroke."

"I'll be home by dinner tomorrow."

In late October of 1943, when Mom had us twins, she told my dad, who was home on leave, that she would need to hire someone to help her with us. As she reported it, he replied condescendingly, "Go ahead, if you want some help."

"*Want* some help! I *need* it!" she retorted, in a post-natal pique.

So, my sister and I were reared by a nanny and a grandmother, as well as by our mom, who returned to teaching after the Christmas holidays. We twins were a package deal in those early years, always together and always dressed alike. Whenever anyone offered to take one of the twins somewhere, the counterpart had to go along. After all, we were twins! Usually in the late afternoon Mom or one of our aunts toted chubby cherubim and sweet seraphim out of the house to give Grandma time to put the finishing touches on the evening meal. On the other hand, our brother, nearly two years older, was often at our dad's house or was taken here and there with adults with much greater ease. As a result, he got out and about a lot more than we did. My guess is that he also got the now-you've-got-to-be-the-man-of-the-family message. He associated with our uncles and grandfathers more than I did. He became assertive and independent as the firstborn often does. Because we twin homebodies had lots of female companionship, many of my fondest childhood memories involve women, frequently one of my grandmothers. Over the years my grandmothers and I developed the unspoken bonds of family members who are each other's favorite. With Grandma Wright that involved Pepper.

During one summer when I was about eleven or twelve, I was walking home at dusk from gardening at Grandma McClelland's house. As I made my way through the long back alley that ran parallel to Main Street, a black puppy began following me. I turned, petted it, and started on my way to 201 again. Looking back, I saw the little shiny-coated pup trotting after me across an intersection. Stooping down, I scooped it up and carried it back to the other side, with it gnawing playfully on my fingers all the while. Discovering it was a "she," I put her down and shooed her away. Scared, she tucked her tail and ran into the surrounding darkness. I started back for home, smiling about the cute little thing as I wiped my fingers dry on my dusty jeans.

Before I knew it, I was tripping over the furball who had made her way back to me lickety-split. When I arrived at our door, I explained that I just couldn't shake my little, black, tag-along companion. Surely, she was lost or abandoned and she looked so hungry that we'd just have to give her something to eat. Grandma consented to letting her stay in the yard on the condition that the stray be sent on her way in the morning.

Well, after playing with her all the next day and smuggling out lots of table scraps, I begged to be able to keep Pepper. After considerable family discussion, I was permitted to keep her, over Grandma's objection. At first, Pepper was confined to the yard. When I let her onto the screened-in porch, Grandma would chase us both out to the yard again. Eventually, however, Pepper had the run of the house, though Grandma objected emptily. Grandma rarely found anything to quibble with me about, except one of Pepper's miscues. No matter what the problem, I would make amends. Through raising Pepper, I learned responsibility: the work and the rewards of taking care of another. She was bright, easy to train, and eager to please. I lavished attention on her.

When fall arrived and we kids returned to school, Pepper and Grandma were left in the house alone. None of us ever knew when the affection began, because for some time Grandma never showed the least interest in the dog when we were around. But, like many of life's ironic commonplaces, Grandma—who had never before been fond of animals—became attached to Pepper.

Grandma's companionship with Pepper deepened as we kids grew up and left home for college or work. One summer when I returned from college, I found that Pepper had been ailing. A checkup showed a large mass of gallstones, and the vet recommended immediate surgery. For several days after the operation, Pepper gradually declined into listlessness. The vet suggested that we take her home and try to revive her in familiar surroundings. I carried her to the porch, where we forced medicine and water on her. Because she was too weak to stand, I would hold her up, trying to help her take a step or two. Every so often, Grandma came to the porch door and watched worriedly; it upset her too much to stay long. Pepper watched us with sad, loving eyes. Phone calls to the vet brought us little encouragement and an offer to end her suffering. After a week of misery for us all, one morning I found Pepper stiffened in rigor mortis. As I carried her out of the house, we were all in tears. While we all grieved that summer, Grandma did so most of all. Some time afterward, I wrote a story called "Pepper to Dust." I no longer recall just how I characterized us and the situation, but despite being maudlin (or perhaps just because it was so), I'm sure it expressed our sense of loss of this latest companion. Of course, Grandma had suffered several losses of family members during her seventy-eight years, including her second son who lived only two days.

Besides our having Pepper in common, during my high school years, when Grandma neared her seventies and her health waned, I moved to a small bedroom off hers, in order to keep an eye on her. When I retired at night, usually she would already be asleep. I would step slowly through the doorway and to her bedside, listening for her breathing. I would pick up the book from her coverlet, mark her place in it, remove her glasses, and turn out her reading lamp. If she happened to be awake when I came in, I'd sit on the side of her bed and we'd chat a bit. Small talk. A favorite dish that she was going to make me tomorrow. Some news from school. A couple of questions about the book she was reading. Then I'd put drops in her eyes and we'd turn in for the night. As I climbed into my bed, I thought that the work of her life was over. I wondered what she looked forward to. But we never talked much beyond the routine activities of the day.

At certain times I intensely wanted to learn Welsh from Grandma, especially when I looked at the Welsh printing on the tribute to her father or when I heard her speak a few words to Mom or Uncle Tom. It was a romantic notion, of course. I thought I could connect with something valuable, thought I could gain some power, if I had command of the language. When I saw the movie *How Green Was My Valley*, I again lit up with the desire to know more about the land, its people, and its language. I hurried to tell Grandma that I had seen the film.

"Oh, that piece of rubbish," she said in disgust.

"What do you mean? It was beautiful," I objected.

"That's what's wrong with it. It looks so beautiful. An ideal picture of the Welsh countryside. But the Wales my folks knew was dirt poor, coal mines, labor struggles, no food on the table. That's why they had to leave."

She splashed cold water on my dewy-eyed face for the moment, but another day a few years later I again entertained idealistic notions. This time they were not so noble and they flaunted my family heritage.

Very late one night, when I drove home for spring vacation during my third year at college, I brought a bottle of wine into our teetotalers' home. In her lifetime, Gram, Grandma's mother, had headed the local group of the Woman's Christian Temperance Union. Mom's three brothers ran the gamut from teetotaler to social drinker to problem drinker. Nobody had ever drunk in our house. I was pouring a glass of wine at the kitchen counter when my sister walked in. She spotted the wine bottle, wheeled around, and shortly returned with Mom, who began with a hostile tone.

"What's the big idea of bringing drink into our home!"

As such messy affairs go, no clear line of reasoning could be discerned in our domestic fracas. We roamed hither, thither, and yon over perceived wrongs, individual failings, and sundry calls to family honor. Our histrionics stopped just short of invoking intercession by the souls of family members who had passed on the other side of the bar, although I was chided that they all must be turning over in their graves at that very instant. My sister remarked sharply that I was in a sophomoric phase of self-righteousness.

Turning to Mom, she said sarcastically, "Poor boy! He's a little slow, so it's taken him an extra year to reach his sophomore period."

Certainly, I did nothing to disprove her when I railed on and on about human hypocrisy, using Mary Jane and Mom as prime examples of Eisenhower Presbyterianism, a brand of social church membership wherein one's highest hope on Sunday morning is that the sermon will end early, so that he can make a one o'clock tee time at the country club. I, on the other hand, contended that I was idealistically striving to live a Christ-centered, sacrificial Christianity. I intoned this point so high-and-mightily. Admittedly, I was slight on the details of this form of sacred living and I was a bit fuzzy on just where underage drinking in our home against Mom's wishes fit. Nonetheless, I distinctly recall making quite a to-do about Jesus changing water into wine at the wedding feast.

Fortunately, we didn't waken Grandma with our noisy debate. However, in my act of defiance, I affronted the values of Grandma's life, too, essentially a more fundamentally sound and time-tested set of values than any of us had. Born Deborah Lloyd Wright on December 17,

1887, in Exeter, Pennsylvania, the middle daughter of Welsh immigrants—a minister-miner and a spunky woman in her second marriage—Grandma was raised according to strict Presbyterian precepts. At eighteen, Grandma married Pop, a young miner, whose immigrant Scotsman father was a brilliant mining engineer and, late in his life, a drunk. Grandma rode out many ups and downs with Pop and then enjoyed, for some years, the elegant lifestyle of the nouveau riche. During this time she suffered the piercing jealousy of her poorer relatives. When Pop lost all of his money in the stock market crash, he began from ground zero again, survived the depression without government assistance, and rebuilt his business, all the while maintaining his position as a powerful local pol. In her life with Pop, Grandma had lost one son in infancy and had raised three other sons and a daughter. Although she lived in a world where male power dominated the scene and she deferred to her husband, she carved out a space that she occupied with dignity. She expressed herself with the spunk and humor of a Welshwoman—even as she endured her husband's ribbing about her countrymen "welshing" on his in the mine wars Up East. And she had lived through two world wars in which her menfolk fought.

She was intensely proud of her family. In her first V-mail to Uncle Ben, when he left for overseas, she told him of Decoration Day activities that young Tommy Dick and others were involved in and wrote with pride, "You just can't keep the Wrights out of the limelight."

When I was growing up at 201, I watched Grandma begin her day with an early-morning cup of tea, loaded with milk and sugar. She set the Lipton teabag aside and reused it several times throughout the day. Cooking large dinners for our family and taking dish after dish to church meals came naturally to her. She had a stock of recipes, many of which came from Gram's boarding-house days. Some she collected through her association with other good cooks in our church family. Written in her own hand in spiral notebooks, Grandma collected dozens of great recipes from her long life in the kitchen. Mary Jane, who has Grandma's fine china and the note-books of recipes, aims to make a book of them. Grandma instilled in all of us kids a love of cooking.

Even though I knew her history and her character, I took Grandma for granted in my late teenage years. Self-centered, I didn't attend to her as I should have.

Three years away from home and being on center stage in several college dramas had given me a big head, even if my mind hadn't been expanded in equal measure by the wisdom of the classical dramatists whose works I performed.

The point of this otherwise pointless act of defiance regarding my family's prohibition against alcohol was to differentiate my new self from my past self. Even if I didn't know who I was—and surely I didn't—I knew I wasn't the unquestioningly obedient boy of my earlier teen years, although even then I could not have qualified as a halo-polishing angel.

On the drive home the next morning to attend Grandma's funeral, I was so troubled because I had had no chance to say a final good-bye to her. I thought about how home wouldn't feel the same without her in it. She had always been there. When I replayed in my mind scenes of our times together, especially those with Pepper, I cried anew so hard that I had to pull off the road and stop. Looking out the windshield down a long, wooded mountain pass in West Virginia, suddenly all of the losses fused together: Pepper, Grandma, and Dad. That great expanse of wilderness mirrored the emptiness inside me. I felt so vulnerable and alone. At the top of my voice I screamed, "Why?" Why did I have to be left so alone? I felt lost on the road. And I would never find my way home again.

19

SPLIT OVER THE VIETNAM WAR

Masontown, Pennsylvania
July 1970

In the mid-sixties, when my brother was living in San Francisco, he visited an army recruiter. Pete had a commercial pilot's license and Uncle Sam wanted pilots for the war in Southeast Asia. The recruiter told Pete that with his commercial license, he would probably be assigned to fly twin Beeches at Fort Ord in California and never even leave the States. Pete wrote to Uncle Ben, telling him that he was thinking of signing up.

Immediately, Uncle Ben dashed off a pencilled note on a sheet of paper from a legal pad: "Do not enlist. This is not a national emergency. Our shores are not threatened." Of course, Uncle Ben was no doubt thinking as much of his sister's welfare as he was of Pete's, knowing how much anguish Mom would live through if Pete followed Dad into the army.

I, too, unhappy in the early years of a marriage quickly souring, contemplated enlisting. Shortly after my grandmother died, I had married, left graduate school, and returned to my alma mater as an English instructor and an assistant dean of men. The job was a boon; the marriage, a mistake. I had been languishing in my graduate studies and the job enabled me to gain insight into the profession and establish solid footing as an educator. In my former English professors and my boss, Dean Fred Kring, I had the best mentors any novice could have. However, my wife and I, who were needy in different ways, had overlooked bad signs in our family histories and had married after a six-month courtship. We soon began suffering from incompatibilities that were compounded by the birth of a child in our second year of marriage. So distraught was I that I often thought of escaping. Once I traveled on impulse to Nantucket, sat on the eastern coast, the farthest edge of the continent, and looked aimlessly into the distant horizon before returning home. At that point an unhappy home was easier to face than an unknowable future alone.

At this time I also visited an army recruiter. I was considering military service as a way out of my marital unhappiness. Opposed to the war, I really couldn't pretend to be answering a patriotic call to arms as my dad had done. Like Pete, I sought Uncle Ben's counsel. He urged me to stay put in my job as an assistant dean and instructor. I did so for a couple of more years before returning for doctoral study.

Several years later, however, as the war in Vietnam wore on, Uncle Ben and I had a decidedly different encounter over it. By that time I had traveled a now-familiar journey with my contemporaries through the degeneration of the jungle war into a political and moral jungle: Nixon and Watergate. The Gulf of Tonkin Resolution. Police riots at the Democratic National Convention in Chicago. President Johnson ordering the bombing of North Vietnam. National Guardsmen shooting four people at Kent State University. American soldiers killing Vietnamese civilians.

Taking a break from graduate school, I visited home and caused an upheaval that fractured our family unity, leaving it in splinters on the living room floor. I must have thought that my generation had invented the use of physical appearance as a political statement. When I arrived at 201 with shoulder-length hair and a beard, I didn't look like my old self to Mom.

"Where's my pretty Benny?"

"Right here under this curly beard."

Uncle Ben sat next to Mom, his daughter, Deb, across the way, and Mary Jane by the porch door.

"You look like one of those hippie protestors." Uncle Ben delivered the line warmly, chuckled, but made his point.

"You know I'm no hippie. But they're right. The war's immoral. American GIs having to kill innocent farmers, women, and children. You and Dad never had to do that."

It was this last line that struck a raw nerve, crossed over a line, launching Uncle Ben into a sermon on the threat of communism in Southeast Asia and the need for patriots to fight to preserve the American way of life. Lord knows, he had earned the right to lecture me on these themes—and a host of others.

Of course, as a young idealist, I still felt right (actually obnoxiously self-righteous) in my position on the war. Yet it hurt, exchanging the first—and only—harsh words with someone I so trusted and admired. Everyone else in the family hurt, too, seeing me so misguided, so lost to our old life together.

20

ANOTHER PARADE, ANOTHER WAR MEMORIAL

Bloomington, Indiana
July 1970

I replayed the recent family fight in my mind as I walked across campus. The rally began where all of Indiana University's political activities originated, in the fabled Dunn Meadow. Set down from the roadway, the meadow is a large grassy, rectangular commons, bounded by an embankment around two sides, the sprawling and exquisite student union building on the third side and a deep woods on the fourth. From a

Quaker I accepted a white armband bearing a black-stenciled peace symbol. I made my way through the crowd to see what I could learn from the speakers who trod to the microphone, one after another. Some spoke perfunctorily, as if merely recording their group present and accounted for. But the radicals—Students for a Democratic Society, conscientious objectors, draft-card burners, and some clerics—spoke fervently, pounding the air with their fists as if hammering swords into ploughshares. Finally, the group was called to march to the square downtown. Climbing the embankment onto the roadway, people fell into a loose formation from curb to curb. Here came the separation of sheep from goats. What had been a gathering of well over two thousand in the sanctuary of the meadow melted away to a few hundred when words gave way to action.

Though a small band, we proceeded buoyantly at first, leaving campus and heading into town to the rhythm of antiwar chants. "Hell no, we won't go!" Word came that stonecutters, positioned on the roadsides near the square, would try to block our approach to the war memorial. We closed ranks, grew quiet, and walked deliberately.

When we reached the cutters, it was like running the gauntlet. They jeered, spit, yelled obscenities, and pumped callused fists in the air, taunting us to come over to where they stood. From the back of a parked pickup, a three-hundred-pounder pointed at one of us longhairs.

"I'll bust your goddam pointy head, you hippie faggot, you!"

University and city police patrolled an invisible corridor between us protestors and the antiprotestors. When we reached the steps of the memorial, a group of cutters roared and lunged off the sidewalk, but the police cut them off, pushing them back as we ascended the steps and circled around the tall statue in the center. "Hell no, we won't go! Hell no, we won't go! Hell no, we won't go!" The Hoosiers who supported the war tried to drown us out with boos and singing.

As we chanted triumphantly, something caught my eye and took my breath away. Here stood a wall of names in gold lettering, some accompanied by gold stars. The argument with my family had been won, so I thought. But now, this seemed so much a personal confrontation with my dad. At this very moment, I felt challenged anew about being on the opposite side of war from him. I never anticipated this emotional attack. It turned my patriotic resolve into a withering query. Was I desecrating hallowed ground by protesting here? Worse, was I betraying my dad's honorable sacrifice? Would he feel the same as Uncle Ben and the family did? Would he be proud of me, or embarrassed, or worse? Amidst the loud choruses, pro and con, in this public square, I wrestled with private drama in silent and excruciating pain, anxiously imploring my dad to understand my position.

21

LEARNING MORE ABOUT
MOM AND DAD

Masontown, Pennsylvania

While the intensity of my need to know more about my dad and his end ebbed and flowed with the vicissitudes of my life, it never totally abated. My first period of real study about the war itself came at about age sixteen, when somehow the burden I felt to be a good son for my dad and my desire to know more about him coalesced. Each night, after doing all of my homework, after eating dinner, and after listening to a Pirates ballgame or watching *The Ed Sullivan Show* or *The*

Lawrence Welk Show or *Kraft Television Theater*, I would turn on my bedside lamp and read a portion of a thick book that Uncle Ben had lent me: *The Rise and Fall of the Third Reich.* Through the pages of this book by foreign correspondent and historian William L. Shirer, I entered a most complex time and place: Hitler's world—the technical achievements, the war machine, the Holocaust. Bad things happened to good people. Good people—and quite a few bad ones—committed cruel, barbarous acts. This was the demonic power my dad had fought to quell. Coming to understand the Nazi ideology, tactics, and zeitgeist, I hoped, would help me gain some peace about my dad's death. But, in this melodramatic period, the more I learned, the more questions were raised, fueling further my obsessive drive to know what happened to him, and to view him as heroic. I imagined all sorts of endings to his life, all violent.

Years later, when the movie about the Battle of the Bulge came out, I felt certain that my dad had been among a truckload of captive GIs who were shot down in cold blood by German machine guns in the middle of a snowy field near Malmédy. Even though a newspaper had once reported this, it amounted to wild speculation, but I needed the certainty of knowing how he died. Besides, this ending made him more tragic, more heroic, in my eyes. And it made me more pathetic, though I thought eminently more pitiable.

Mom's death in April 2000, after a long illness, brought a flood of new information and, with it, the surfacing of long-suppressed feelings. This next period of intense study began with some of Mom's effects, documents about Dad, supplying knowledge that I had lived without for so long. The absence of such information over the years had created more than a void. The emptiness of not knowing filled up with uncertainties, questions, inferences, worries.

Newspaper clippings, telegrams, personal letters, and War Department documents—browned and brittle with age—provided hints about my family's tragedy. It's my nature to try to piece things together, to understand the larger meaning that is the sum of so many smaller things. Thus, from reading these several documents and from talking with family members, I envisioned scenes at the heart of my family's tragedy, scenes in the trauma that Mom suffered first and most of all:

DECEMBER 1944

"Marianna, there's a telegram. You better sit down to read it."

As she rips the envelope, tears are already dropping on it.

"He's been missing in action since the seventeenth. Oh, my God!"

Later at the Christmas Eve service in the First Presbyterian Church word spreads that Pete McClelland is missing in Germany.

"Good heavens! After three years of puttin' in for overseas. Now this."

"They kept him training big equipment operators during his first hitch. He just reupped in October. Got into the 589th Artillery outfit, shootin' a howitzer."

"He ain't been over there but a month."

"And Marianna with them three kids. Little Petie ain't three yet. How old are the twins?"

"Just turned a year old. Good thing she's got her family."

"Yeah, but what about Ben and Tom? They're still over there."

"So's Pete's brother Jim."

JANUARY 1945

For weeks Mom knew little more. She desperately sought information from the government. Bits of news came out, weeks after the events, telling, at once, too little and more than she wanted to hear. Just a scrap of an article from the Uniontown, Pennsylvania, *Herald-Gazette* remains to show what news Mom read. Entitled "Tales of Heroism by the 106th Division," the article reported that in "two days regiments and supporting artillery and armor of the Golden Lion Division were wiped out. In those two days the men of the two regiments were engulfed by the overwhelming weight of Field Marshal Von Rundstedt's breakthrough spearhead. They went down fighting."

With the D-Day assault behind them and the Germans on the run, Mom must have wondered how such an incredible turn of events could happen. She must have been worried sick over my dad's fate: Was he lying in the freezing mud dead or, worse, wounded and suffering? Was he captured? Was he being treated well or tortured?

Two letters from my dad, handwritten just days before the battle, arrived sometime during this period, surely intensifying Mom's anguish. The son he addresses in the second letter is my older brother, Pete.

SAT. 10 DEC 44

Dear Marianna,

Your breath will be coming in pants after you read these next few lines. To begin with, my hands are quite cold consequently, this writing may not be too legible.

I have been to France and while there I had the opportunity to visit Le Havre & Rouen also quite a few others too insignificant to mention. The French certainly show the strain of war. Most everyone trys to beg your rations. Cigarettes, candy & gum top the list.

At the present time I'm in Belgium. My impression is that they want to remain Belgian, but they are sympathetic to the Germans. They dislike Hitler. We are situated in a wooded area which gives us a lot of protection from air observation. There is also a foot of snow which helps camaflouge.

I don't mind the cold too much. I have a good sleeping bag & several blankets. I would welcome a muffler & and a pair of leather lined mittens. I'll write Petey [sic] Dick a letter in a few days. I don't know when I'll get to see Tom, Ben or Jim.

Love,

Pete

TUES. 12 DEC 44

Somewhere in Germany

Dear Son,

Several weeks ago I was in England, but since leaving the Isle, I have traveled beyond the German border. Today I visited the battery positions therefore I was within several miles of the front lines.

We are living, at present, in a German farmhouse. Inside this joint, we have the furniture, that was used by the previous occupants, at our disposal. Tile lined bathrooms & and kitchens are very useful. However, the water supply isn't 100% efficient as yet, but we are working on it.

LATER

Dear Marianna,

Three more days & our fourth anniversary will have arrived. I'll never regret that day because I married the best girl I ever knew & and she has become one wonderful mother. I'll never be able to compete with you for the kids affection. The wedding band is making quite a mark on my finger. Time wasn't available for me to get you a decent xmas present.

Love,
Pete

I can only imagine Mom's heartbreak at reading those letters. It was years before more definitive reports shed some light on my dad's last days. The Army Education Services issued a memorial booklet to former members of the 106th Infantry Division and their families. Mom received one. Written with the assistance of Commanding Officer Donald A. Stroh and his staff, the booklet, printed in italics, narrates the battle engagement with military detail and rhetoric suited to a commemorative history:

> **DEC. 16, 1944:** Springing from the bleak vastness of the Schnee Eifel with the speed of a coiled snake, Field Marshal von Rundstedt's desperate but mighty counter-offensive struck toward Belgium and the Ardennes. Carefully hoarded Panther and Tiger tanks, followed by crack, battle-tested infantry, launched the last-chance gamble aimed at shattering the taut lines of the US First Army, seizing the cities of Liege and Antwerp and slashing through the Allied forces to the sea.
>
> The full force of this massive attack was thrown against the new, untried 106th Infantry Division which had gone to the front lines for the first time only five days previous. . . .
>
> Treetops snapped like toothpicks under murderous shell bursts. Doughs burrowed into their foxholes and fortifications, waited tensely for the attack which would follow.

The darkness was filled with bursts from medium and heavy field pieces plus railway artillery which had been shoved secretly into position. The explosions were deafening and grew into a terrifying hell of noise when Nazis started using their "Screaming Meemies."

Full weight of the barrage was brought to bear on the 589th F[ield] A[rtillery] B[attlio]n, supporting the 422nd. Hundreds of rounds blasted their positions in 35 minutes.

At 0700 the barrage lifted in some forward areas, although St. Vith remained under fire. Now came the attack. Waves of Volksgrenadiers, spearheaded by panzer units, smashed against the division's line in a desperate try for a decisive, early breakthrough. They were stopped. A second attack was thrown against the division. Again, the 106th doughs held. Nazis threw in wave after wave of fresh troops, replacing their losses. There were no replacements for the 106th.

Lionmen settled to their grim business, dug deeper, fought with everything they had. German bodies piled up, often at the very rim of the defenders' foxholes. Still the Nazis came.

All during the day the attacks mounted in fury. Hundreds of fanatical Germans rushed straight toward the American lines, only to be mowed down or driven back by a hail of steel. Others came on, met the same fate. The deadly, careful fire of the stubborn defenders exacted a dreadful toll on the Wehrmacht.

Finally, under pressure of overwhelming numbers, the 14th Cavalry Group was forced to withdraw on the north flank, giving the Germans their first wedge in the division front. Enemy tanks and infantry in increasing numbers then hacked at the slowly widening gap in an effort to surround the 422nd.

In the meantime, a second tank-led assault, supported by infantry and other panzers, hammered relentlessly at the 423rd and 424th. Early next morning a wedge was driven between the two regiments. This southern German column then swung north to join the one that had broken through in the 14th's sector. . . .

Two regiments, the 422nd and the 423rd, with the 589th and 590th, F[ield] A[rtillery] B[attlio]ns, were cut off and surrounded by the sheer weight and power of the concentrated German hammer blows. . . .

Surrounded, the 422nd and 423rd fought on. Ammunition and food ran low. Appeals were radioed to H[ead] Q[uarters] to have supplies flown in, but the soupy fog which covered the frozen countryside made air transport impossible.

The two encircled regiments regrouped early Dec. 18 for a counter-attack aimed at breaking out of the steel trap. This bold thrust was blocked by sheer weight of German soldiers.

The valiant stand of the two fighting regiments inside the German lines was proving to be a serious obstacle to Nazi plans. It forced von Rundstedt to throw additional reserves into the drive to eliminate the surrounded Americans, enabled the remaining units and their reinforcements to prepare the heroic defense of St. Vith, delayed the attack schedule and prevented the early stages of the Battle of the Bulge from exploding into a complete German victory.

Low on ammunition, food gone, ranks depleted by three days and nights of ceaseless in-fighting, the 422nd and 423rd battled on from their foxholes and old Siegfried Line bunkers. They fought the evergrowing horde of panzers with bazookas, rifles and machine guns. One of their last radio messages was, "Can you get some ammunition through?"

Then, no more was heard from the two encircled regiments except what news was brought back by small groups and individuals who escaped the trap. Many were known to have been killed. Many were missing. Many turned up later in German prison camps.

Mom could have known very little of this story at the time. Then, on the twenty-fifth of January, she received the dreaded telegram confirming Dad's death. Two days later a letter of sympathy arrived, stating some very painful details.

WAR DEPARTMENT
THE ADJUTANT GENERAL'S OFFICE

WASHINGTON 25, D.C.
IN REPLY TO
AG 201 McClelland, Ewing R.
PC-N 017108
27 January 1945
Mrs. Marianna W. McClelland
201 North Main Street
Masontown, Pennsylvania

Dear Mrs. McClelland:

It is with deep regret that I am writing to confirm the recent telegram informing you of the death of your husband, First Lieutenant Ewing R. McClelland, 0426588, Field Artillery, who was previously reported missing in action since 17 December 1944 in Germany.

Information has now been received from the German Government through the International Red Cross stating that your husband died on 23 December 1944 in a prisoner of war camp, and it is alleged that his death was due to an air attack. It has been officially recorded that he was killed in action on 23 December 1944.

I realize the burden of anxiety that has been yours and deeply regret the sorrow this report brings you. May the knowledge that he made the supreme sacrifice for his home and country be a source of sustaining comfort.

I extend to you my deepest sympathy.
Sincerely yours,
J.A. ULIC

Major General,
The Adjutant General

Mom tried to get more information about the circumstances of my dad's death, but to no avail. Eight months after receiving the letter from the War Department, she wrote to an old friend in New York, Dr. H. B. Hill, from Camp Lee days, inquiring why she hadn't heard from anyone who had been overseas with Dad. He replied, "The reason that you have not received any news directly from anyone with Pete must be attributed to the fact that the survivors, if any, must be under great difficulty to obtain addresses." He went on to offer his condolences and his estimate of my dad: "You probably know that I thought the world of Pete. I admired and respected him very much. I enjoyed working with him as well as the times when we were 'off duty.' I also know that the officers and men of the Third Battalion had the same opinion of him as I did. I know that Col. Batson and I talked about Pete on several occasions even after we left Camp Lee. It was our opinion that he was the finest junior officer in our group and we both regretted that Pete was not assigned to Camp Robinson with us. . . . Pete was impatient to get back into the artillery. He thought his time was wasted in the medical group. In my opinion he was a very valuable leader and would make a success of any assignment."

A separate Battle Casualty Report, issued by the War Department, cited the place of my dad's death as Stalag 12A. Located at Limburg, several miles inside Germany, north of Frankfurt, Stalag 12A served as a transit camp; "its facilities were insufficient for handling the thousands of Allied ground troops captured on the Western Front." After some days of bone-wearying travel my dad and his comrades crowded into a place where already "the GIs had to fight other desperate Americans for living space, and were compelled to remain vigilant to retain their food and clothing." Their survival in this hellhole ended abruptly on December 23, when the overcast skies cleared, bringing an Allied strafing and bombing attack in which my dad and many others perished.

Along with thousands of other American dead from that costly battle, my dad was quickly buried in Diez, Germany. Later their remains were disinterred and placed in an American cemetery in The Netherlands, near where they had fallen.

Some years after the war Mom made a further attempt to get government records about Dad's service and death. Apparently, she needed information in order to complete some newly arrived forms for survivor's benefits. Because Uncle Ben was living in Washington, D.C., and working for the FBI, she had him request that several documents be sent on to her from the War Department. We children knew about none of this during our early years. Because were so young, we did not know our dad. We did not learn how he died: "prisoner of war," "his death was due to an air attack." We did not experience losing him. We did not undergo the painful and cathartic process of grieving with our mom and family. By the time I was old enough to ask questions, the adults said very little, never revealing any specifics. Undoubtedly, they wanted to spare me the pain that they had felt. And did not want to rekindle their own grief.

But for me the emptiness, the not knowing, was itself a painful reality. It was not just that I was growing up without a father, but rather that I was growing up in the shadow of a war hero father's death, a ghost that floated in and out of my consciousness. Not knowing who he was affected my sense of who I was. Uncertainties, questions, speculations about his identity and mine dogged me for over fifty years.

Among my dad's things that Mom had kept, we discovered after her death, was the wedding band she had given him when they eloped, the one he mentioned in his last letter home. Returned to her inside an envelope labeled "Personal Effects" from the Army Effects Bureau of the War Department, the simple silver band with a ridge around its center is sealed in thick yellow cellophane and stapled to a piece of cardboard. No longer a true circle, the band appears to have been compressed slightly into an oval shape. As I looked at the ring, I imagined the experience of his final days.

The thunderous predawn artillery assault flashing like lightning in the cold dark sky; the horrible firefight in the snow-covered Ardennes forest; the frenzied, attempted retreat; the stunning capture of two whole battalions; the forced march along muddy roads to the already-overcrowded Stalag 12A at Limburg, Germany; the deprivation and degradation of imprisonment in inhumane conditions. And, finally, the violent terror of the Allied strafing and bombing attack.

As I think about that very moment of my dad's death, I wonder, Why did he have to die? Why did fate put him in just that spot at just that time? More pragmatic questions also arise: How did he fare in those dire conditions in his final days? Just how did he die? What were his final thoughts? While it is painful for me to think about his death, and while I will never be able to answer those questions definitively, addressing them has brought me a sense of connection with him. Learning more about Dad's last days has not only shown me how he died but has also led me to believe that, to the bitter end, he was ever mindful of us—those for whom he died.

22

PILGRIMAGE

Utrecht, en route to Margraten, The Netherlands
August 2000

In piecing together my dad's story, I now make an important journey, as my brother did before me, a pilgrimage to Europe to visit my dad's grave at the American Military Cemetery near Margraten, The Netherlands.

My wife, my niece, a good friend, and I board the train at two in the afternoon. We pass out of this college town with its medieval heritage. We sip Cokes, eat snacks, and talk easily. But the journey, a long-awaited pilgrimage, is at the back of my mind.

I see those parentheses, that gold star. I smell those mothballs.

Amsterdam is just down the track. It's filled with backpacking students, a dizzying number of bicycles, and grass. Cafés spill onto sidewalks. Vacationers eat and drink, and smoke endlessly.

South of Amsterdam, farm after look-alike farm passes in the window. Under cloudy skies sheep and cattle graze in small pastures bounded by deep, water-filled ditches.

We arrive at and depart punctually from industrial sections of fair-sized cities and from edges of small towns, ringed by well-tended garden plots.

So, this is Holland. Land of sturdy wooden shoes. Land of great rounds of cheese.

But for me, land of the living dead. Off and on for over fifty years I've peered into those parentheses. I've stared at that gold star. I've smelled those mothballs. He was captured, killed, and buried in Europe. He rose again from the dead in my recurring questions and theories about his short life and its violent end.

During the two-hour ride, I thumb through pages printed from the Internet, pausing to look at the gauzy picture of the American Military Cemetery. The train wends its way to the country's southernmost region, a jutting finger of land bordered on the east by Belgium and on the west by Germany.

At Maastricht, a typical Mercedes taxi makes the seven-kilometer trip westward to Margraten. At the cemetery entrance the engraved inscription on the exterior wall, taken from General Dwight D. Eisenhower's dedication of the Golden Book in St. Paul's Cathedral in London, reads:

> HERE WE AND ALL WHO SHALL HEREAFTER
>   LIVE IN FREEDOM
> WILL BE REMINDED THAT TO THESE MEN
>   AND THEIR COMRADES
> WE OWE A DEBT TO BE PAID WITH GRATEFUL
>   REMEMBRANCE
> OF THEIR SACRIFICE AND WITH THE HIGH
>   RESOLVE
> THAT THE CAUSE FOR WHICH THEY DIED
>   SHALL LIVE

A Dutch attendant greets us warmly, almost reverentially. He graciously offers sympathy for our loss, eagerly provides computer-printed data on our "family member," carefully outlines the history of the cemetery, and slowly but purposefully leads us toward the gravesite.

My brother, Pete, made this visit, alone, a dozen or more years ago. He took pictures for us. I don't recall questioning him about anything but physical details of the area. And he remained his stoical self. Now, I wonder what he thought when he viewed this scene.

The skies have cleared and the late-afternoon sun slants at our backs. We walk along the rectangular reflecting pool of the Court of Honor past still more engraved memorial statements about bravery and honor and gratitude.

> IN MEMORY
> OF
> THE VALOR
> AND THE
> SACRIFICES
> WHICH
> HALLOW THIS GROUND

The side of a building displays three maps in bright blues and greens. Captions provide a historical outline of the progress of the Allied victory in the closing months of the war. Dates. Place names. Troop units. Strategic and tactical moves. I search for information about how the three thousand Americans buried here died. Just where was this costly skirmish? What maneuvers led to my dad's capture? Understandably, the narrative focuses on the successful battles that eventually thwart the German counteroffensive, providing no details about the lost battles.

Ahead of us, a 101-foot-high memorial tower bears this inscription, a free translation of Pericles's oration, as recorded by Thucydides:

> EACH FOR HIS OWN MEMORIAL
> EARNED PRAISE THAT WILL NEVER DIE
> AND WITH IT
> THE GRANDEST OF ALL SEPULCHRES
> NOT THAT IN WHICH
> HIS MORTAL BONES ARE LAID
> BUT A HOME
> IN THE MINDS OF MEN

Climbing the steps from the memorial to the graves, I feel it coming. Arriving at the top of the steps, I see for the first time the vast expanse of brilliant white crosses in a verdant sea of grass.

The scene carries me back to Kennedy's funeral at Arlington. There's no mass of mourners here today, no flag-draped caisson in a cortege, no riderless horse with boots backwards in the stirrups, no Black Watch bagpipe players, no national day of grief. But when I survey the expanse of the cemetery and consider the extent of individual commitment, the feelings of that day come back to me. The sense that our world has been so diminished by a dear loss. The belief that this moment helps me define better what it is to be an American. The desire—in the face of this sacrifice—to be as good, to count for as much, as I can.

Walking deliberately into Plot J, to the middle of Row 3, I stand at Grave 8. It hits hard now. The others stand back respectfully. From the myriad of anonymous crosses, I look through the memory of that gold star and those mothballs and parentheses to the single white marble cross:

EWING R. MC CLELLAND
1LT 589 FA BN 106 DIV
PENNSYLVANIA DEC 23 1944

I bow my head and pray to his memory, giving thanks for the life he made possible for us. As I open my eyes and look at the stark white stone cross again, the emotion erupts from within. Never mind that it's old family history. It doesn't matter that his remains have been here for nearly fifty-six years. It doesn't matter that I never knew him. Wait.

Yes, in fact, it does. It is just because I have no direct memory of him. It's precisely because I have had no grave to visit. It's owing directly to the uncertain memories of what others told about him that creates the overwhelming emotional impact.

All of the questions that I still hold inside collide in a convulsing emptiness. For the first time I cry, sob, shaking. I turn and accept my wife's comforting.

Later, my niece and I place flowers on the grave and take pictures for the rest of the family. For the first time she tells me that, looking at a picture of her grandfather once, she recognized the shape of her own hand in his.

"That's my hand, too," she shouts, replaying the scene for me. "Who was he? Why was I robbed of knowing my grandfather?" Her questions are the living testimony of thousands of family members, I realize, the survivors who pay the daily interest on the costly sacrifice of their forefathers.

For a moment I am able to get outside of my personal focus to realize something of what she and other family members have been dealing with. Slowly, we retrace our steps out of the cemetery, linger to reread the memorials, then reboard the taxi and leave my dad in his resting place, undisturbed, but no longer unvisited.

23

REACHING A MILESTONE

Oxford, Mississippi

Since returning from Europe, I have been trying to take in all that transpired in that brief visit. Standing before him in his grave made the loss more palpable. Now I can say that I've been there with him. I saw the memorial to him. I acknowledged his sacrifice for me, indeed for all of us for whom he died. The pilgrimage enabled me to grieve, to begin healing, and to gain another view on my dad's identity—as well as a better grasp on mine.

It also motivated me to learn more about his life and his death. On one research trip to my hometown, I visited a man who had been stationed at the same army base as my dad. I expected Mr. Olenik to tell me some interesting stories about his card-playing days with Dad, but his first words took me by surprise: "Your dad should have never died. He didn't have to go. That was his own fault. I didn't go and I'm still alive to tell about it."

When I sat down across the kitchen table from him, Mr. Olenik explained. Sure, he and Dad had played cards together. Of course, as an officer, Dad had had privileges that Mr. Olenik, an enlisted man, didn't have, such as going to the Officers' Club. He called my dad a "gung ho" type.

"Not me," he said. "You know, there's a saying in the army. If they ask volunteers to take one step forward, you step back." He continued, "One night your dad comes to my barracks with a bunch of other men.

"'Say, men,' your dad starts out, 'all of us have decided to put in for overseas. Will you go with us?' A lot of guys say, 'Sure, we're with you, Pete.' But I tell him I wasn't puttin' in for nothin'.

"'You're gonna be the only one not goin,'" your dad says. And I tell him, 'And I'll still be here when you guys come back in boxes.' And that was the truth. Those guys shouldn't have gone."

Leaving Mr. Olenik's home, I was unsettled by what he had told me. I had not wanted to hear such words as the epilogue to my dad's life. Reflecting further, however, I realized that Dad was a willing participant in his era's zeitgeist. He wouldn't have wanted to survive if it had meant being a slacker. He voluntarily put himself at risk to protect us and our way of life. Dad was the kind of man who took one step forward. He was the kind of husband Mom could respect, a father of whom we could be proud.

Back home, as I think more and more often about Mom and Dad, they both become more real to me. And I feel more a part of them.

I remove a rusty staple, slit the thick, yellowed cellophane, and slide the ring out. It takes some effort to clear the knuckle and it fits snugly. I wonder how long it will take to make a mark on my finger, too.

EPILOGUE

Oxford, Mississippi

What does recalling the scenes and people of my life mean to me now? As a person out of the Wright-McClelland heritage who is facing an entirely different world from that of my mom and dad, and our forebears, I choose to understand certain things from this history.

I feel the loss of that heritage, of that culture, of that world and its time; and I feel the loss of the individual family members who raised me. They are all gone now, as gone as my dad always was to me.

On the other hand, in composing this recollection of life stories with them, I have been reliving our time together and have brought them powerfully to mind, which has enabled me to see and hear them again. My family—my dad, especially—is alive to me now more than ever.

Reviewing my family, I have taken my own measure, redefined my own identity, become more than the man I was. If I feel as though I am taller now and can see farther, it is because I stand on their shoulders. Moreover, from them as examples, from their sacrifices, from their nurturing care, and from an understanding they gave me of their world—of our shared heritage passed on through storytelling—I carry into my world renewed strength to contend with its challenges and vicissitudes.